MAPPING IDEAS

SAYED ATHAR ALI HASHMI

MEER CORP.
PUBLICATION

ISBN: 9798534569261

Author	**Sayed Athar Ali Hashmi**
Editor	**Amir Hashmi**
Published by	**Meer Corporation™ Publication**
Permission Inquiries	hashmi_athar@hotmail.com
Publication Inquiries	meercare@live.com

©2021 All rights reserved. Sayed Athar Ali Hashmi

Sayed Athar Ali Hashmi asserts the moral right to be identified as the author of this work. This book is entirely a work of study. The names, characters, and incidents portrayed in it are the product of the study and various relevant studies conducted by the author. The publication sold under the condition that, it is not by way of trade or otherwise, be lent, resold, hired out, circulated, and no reproduction in any form, in whole or in part except for brief quotations in critical articles or reviews I may be made without written permission of the publishers. The work is solely used for educational purposes, without the prior written permission of the copyright owner that is the author, any part of this book not to be reproduced, distributed, or transmitted in any form or by any means, whether electronic/digital or print or mechanical/physical, or stored in information storage or retrieval system.

ABOUT THE AUTHOR

SAYED ATHAR ALI HASHMI
BCA, MCA, PGDCA, M.Phil. (Computer Science)

Sayed Athar Ali Hashmi is an Indian IT Author specialization in Computer Programming and GIS. Started career as programmer, and has more than a decade of experience as a Professor, and an Author. His books have received starred reviews by academic student and scholars. The author graduated masters in Computer Applications (MCA) from National Institute of Technology (NIT), Raipur, and M.Phil. (Computer Science) from Dr. CV Raman University, Chhattisgarh.

DISCLAIMER

This book is meant for educational and learning purposes. The author of the book has taken all reasonable care to ensure that the contents of the book do not violate any copyright or other intellectual property rights of any person in any manner whatsoever. In the event, the author has been unable to track any source and if any copyright has been inadvertently infringed, please notify the publisher in writing for any corrective action. Every effort has been made to ensure that there are no errors or omissions of any kind. Even after this, inform us if there is any error, inaccuracy, or discrepancy so that it does not have an antecedent in the upcoming edition. All disputes are subject to the jurisdiction of competent courts in Dhamtari, Chhattisgarh only. It is specifically advised that its publisher, author, or vendor will not be liable for any loss or damage arising from or related to the content. Respected readers are urged to match the entire publication of this book with the official publications or notifications to prevent any kind of doubt.

PREFACE

This book is designed for all the fundamentals of the Geodatabase; creating and managing the geodatabase, using domains, subtypes and topology to better manage your data, using images with the geodatabase, and using specialized editing tools to correct and clean data. In this valuable book, you'll learn how to use Geodatabases by working through a project. The project is preparing data for an area and working with data analyze information. This course assumes you are comfortable with using ArcGIS 10 for general GIS tasks and that you have had some editing experience.

The book is dedicatedly designed for the basics of creating and managing a Geodatabase, and then converting data to the geodatabase format. The fundamental of database and its model, how to design database, database models and database schema. Designing schema for geodatabase, built up the designed data base, and sample extension that will make it easier to manage and create reports on your geodatabase.

CONTENTS

Introduction 17
    1.1 Course Introduction 17
1.2 Introduction to geo – spatial Data 18
    1.2.1 What is geodata? 18
    1.2.2 What is geo spatial data? 18
    1.2.3 What is geodatabase? 18
    1.2.4 Pre requirement for the course 19
    1.2.5 Software required for the course 19
1.2.6 Before you start 20
    Georeferencing 20
    Digitization 20
    Editing 21
    Query 21
1.3 Introduction to geodatabase 22
    1.3.1 Spatial reference 24
    1.3.2 Spatial index and grid size 25
    1.3.3 Field properties 25
    1.3.4 Default field properties 25
    1.3.5 Field precision and scale 26
    1.3.6 Required fields 26
    1.3.7 Field, table, and feature class aliases 26
    1.3.8 Tracking properties of geometry 28

1.3.9 Feature datasets 28

1.3.10 Topologies..28

1.3.11 Geometric networks 29

1.3.12 Relationship classes 29

1.4 Practical – Getting Started 31

1.4.1 Getting started with ArcGIS 31

1.4.2 Understands ArcMap 32

ArcCatalog..32

ArcToolbox 33

Table of contents Window...34

Setting up default geodtabase....................................36

2. Geodatabase Design 39

2.1 Conceptual Design 39

2.1.1 Identify key information layers...........................39

2.1.2 Specify scale ranges and spatial representation:40

2.1.3 Group representation into datasets 40

2.2 Logical Design Phase 40

2.2.1 Define database structure and behaviour 41

2.2.2 Define spatial properties....................................42

2.3 Physical Design Phase 43

2.3.1 Implement design 43

2.3.2 Design building and maintaining work flows 44

2.3.3 Document your design.......................................45

2.4 Things to be consider before designing geodatabase
....47

3. Software Analyses Tools for GIS 49
　3.1 Introduction 49
　3.2 Geospatial Tools..49
　3.3 Advantages of GIS tool...51
　3.4 Commercial Off The Shelf (COTS) 52
　3.4.1 ArcGIS..53
　3.4.2 ERDAS IMAGTNE 54
　3.4.3 Envi..55
　3.5 Free hand open source software (FOSS) 56
　3.5.1 Usage and functionality 57
　3.5.2 Examples 57
　3.5.2.1 Grass GIS 57
　3.5.2.2 Quantum GIS..58
　3.6 Hardware requirements and constraints...............59
4.1 DBMS (Database Management System)....................61
　4.1 Data definition language...61
　4.2 Data dictionary..62
　4.3 Data-entry module...62
　4.4 Data update model 62
　4.5 Report generator 62
　4.6 Query language...62
　4.7 Architecture of DBMS:..63
　4.9 Database models 65
　4.10 Practical 69

4.10.1 Creating database in MS Access 69

4.10.2 Create a table 69

4.10.3 Export access database to MS Excel 73

5 Geodatabase 75

5.1 What is geodatabase and spatial data? 75

5.2 Spatial data 75

5.3 Why to use geodatabase 76

5.4 What is the geodatabase? 77

5.5   Types of geodatabase 78

5.5.1 File 78

5.5.2 Personal 78

5.5.3 Multiuser geodatabase 79

5.6 Architecture of geodatabase 79

5.6.1 Information Model 79

5.6.2 The application layer 80

5.6.3 Transaction model 80

5.7 Components of geodatabase 80

5.7.1 Raster 80

5.7.2 Vector 80

5.7.3 Coverages 80

5.7.4 Terrain 81

5.7.5 Annotation 81

5.8 Structure of geodatabase 81

5.8.1 Geodatabase storage in tables and files 82

5.8.2 Advanced geographic data types extend feature classes, raster, and attribute tables 83

6.1 Defining feature class 85

6.2 Creating data type for feature class 88

6.3 feature class data type 88

6.3.1 Numeric Data type 88

6.3.1 Integers 89

6.3.1.2 Float 90

6.3.2 Text 92

6.3.3 Date 92

6.3.4 Blob 92

6.3.5 Guid 93

6.3.6 Raster datatype 94

6.3.6.1 Dataset 94

6.3.6.2 Raster catalog 95

6.3.6.3 An attribute of type raster 97

7. FIELD WORK 98

7.1 Ground control point collection 98

7.2 Use of base map 98

7.2 Defining data 99

7.3 Methodology used 99

7.3.1 GENERAL 99

7.3.2 TIME MANAGEMENT AND COVERAGE 100

7.3.3 DATA ORGANIZATION 101

8. Building geodatabase 102

8.1 Creating Geodatabase and Feature dataset 102

8.2 Creating Feature class..110

8.2.1 Creating a feature class in a feature dataset 112

8.2.2 Creating Standalone feature class 115

8.2.3 Feature Class Representation 118

8.2.4 Creating a new feature class by saving the contents of a map layer in ArcMap..124

8.2.4 Copying Schema...125

8.2.5 Modifying field data types 130

9. Migrating your existing data into the Geodatabase ..134

9.1 Importing data into the geodatabase 134

9.2 Exporting data into the geodatabase...................135

9.3 Migrating Shapefiles into a Geodatabase 137

9.3.1 Feature class to feature class.............................137

9.3.2 Feature class to geodatabase 139

10. Joins and Relates...140

10.1 Rational for Using Related Tables 140

10.2 Cardinalities in Relations....................................140

10.3 Types of File associations in ArcGIS 141

10.4 Special Features of Joins in ArcGIS.....................142

10.5 Other Types of File associations Supported by ArcGIS Other ArcGIS...142

10.5 Join and relating tables 143

10.6 Joining the attributes from a table 144

10.6.1 One-to-one and many-to-one relationships...145

10.6.2 One-to-many and many-to-many relationships 146

10.7 Practical – Joining Table......................................147

11. Annotations in geodatabase 150

11.1 What is annotation? 150

11.2 Types of annotation..150

11.2.1 Standard annotation......................................150

11.2.2 Feature-linked annotation.............................151

11.2.3 Dimension annotation 152

11.3 Creating annotations 153

11.3.1 Creating annotation feature class...................153

11.3.2 Creating Annotation features 158

11.3.3 Convert labels to annotation 160

12. Network Analyses 162

12.1 The Network Analyst..162

12.2 Network Dataset...163

12.3 Multimodal network dataset.............................165

12.4 Exercise 166

Introduction

1.1 Course Introduction

This course is designed to show students all the fundamentals of the Geodatabase; creating and managing the geodatabase, using domains, subtypes and topology to better manage your data, using images with the geodatabase, and using specialized editing tools to correct and clean data.

Students will learn how to use Geodatabases by working through a project. The project is preparing data for an area and working with data analyze information.

This course assumes you are comfortable with using ArcGIS 10 for general GIS tasks and that you have had some editing experience.

- In the first section we will look at the basics of creating and managing a Geodatabase, and then converting data to the geodatabase format.

- In the second section, we'll cover the fundamental of database and its model, how to design database, database models and database schema. Then we will design schema for geodatabase

- In the third section, you will built up the designed data base

- In the last module, we'll show you a sample extension that will make it easier to manage and create reports on your geodatabase. Student will make a project. This project will be based on the course and will be considered as there achievement. A sample map is shown next page.

1.2 Introduction to geo – spatial Data

1.2.1 What is geodata?

Geodata is information about geographic locations that is stored in a format that can be used with a geographic information system (GIS). Geodata can be stored in a database, geodatabase, shapefile, coverage, raster image, or even a dbf table or Microsoft Excel spreadsheet.

1.2.2 What is geo spatial data?

Geospatial data or geographic information it is the data (or information) that recognizes the on Earth, such as terrain features, boundaries and more. Spatial data is usually stored as coordinates and topology, and is data that can be mapped. Spatial data is often accessed, manipulated or analyzed through Geographic Information Systems (GIS).

1.2.3 What is geodatabase?

Definition by ESRI: Geodatabase is a collection of geographic datasets for use by ArcGIS. There are various types of geographic datasets, including feature classes, attribute tables, raster datasets, network datasets, topologies and many others.

1.2.4 Pre requirement for the course

The primary goal of the program is to ensure that students become sufficiently grounded in theoretical underpinnings of GIS to make informed use of existing GIS applications and gain skills needed to construct new applications in the physical or social realms. The full range of GIS capabilities is covered, including data capture, analysis, and modeling and cartographic representation.

The program covers the foundations of GIS and spatial analysis, including cartography and statistical methods. Through hands-on exposure in the form of lab exercises, course projects, and an internship or independent project, experience will be acquired with major GIS software packages, including ArcGIS. By teaching concepts and hands-on use, the program differs from a typical short course designed for GIS training in a particular software package.

The program is intended to serve:

- Who wish to acquire technical expertise to support the topical knowledge gained in their undergraduate major
- Who wish to acquire specialized training to meet current (or future) job requirements calling for GIS knowledge

1.2.5 Software required for the course

In this course we are using ArcGIS 10 to build and manage geographic information using features and tabular data, imagery, and geodatabase.

1.2.6 Before you start

Georeferencing

To Georeference means to associate something with locations in physical space. The term is commonly used in the geographic information systems field to describe the process of associating a physical map or raster image of a map with spatial locations. Georeferencing may be applied to any kind of object or structure that can be related to a geographical location, such as points of interest, roads, places, bridges, or buildings.

Geographic locations are most commonly represented using a coordinate reference system, which in turn can be related to a geodetic reference system such as WGS-84.

Digitization

Digitizing, the process of converting features into a digital format, is one way to create data. There are several ways to digitize new features. These include digitizing "on-screen" or "heads up" over an image, digitizing a hard copy of a map on a digitizing board, or using automated digitization.

Interactive, or heads up digitization, is one of the most common methods. In this method, you display an aerial photograph, satellite image, or orthophotograph on-screen as a basemap, then you draw features, such as roads, buildings, or parcels, on top of it.

Editing

ArcGIS allows you to create and edit several kinds of data. You can edit feature data stored in shapefiles and geodatabases, as well as various tabular formats. This includes points, lines, polygons, text (annotations and dimensions), multipatches, and multipoints. You can also edit shared edges and coincident geometry using topologies and geometric networks.

Query

Handout is useful for memorizing the feasibility study, survey and analysis that you perform for the geodatabase. You need to record all the information before you design your geodatabase. Information that you collect on paper (handout) will be consider as rules. This rules will be implemented to your geodatabase design.

One of the most important steps in creating an effective database is designing its schema. The same is true for any geodatabase. When designing a geodatabase, you should consider questions

- What kind of data will be stored in the database?
- In what projection do you want your data stored?
- Do you want to establish rules about how the data can be modified?
- How do you want to organize your object classes and subtypes?
- Do you want to maintain special relationships between objects of different types?
- Will your database contain networks?

- Will your database store custom objects?

Once you have answered these and other questions, you are ready to begin creating your geodatabase design. You can use the data modeling guidelines in this book to help you design a geodatabase which both meets your requirements and also performs well. This book will then guide you through the process of physically implementing your geodatabase design.

1.3 Introduction to geodatabase

Geodatabases organize geographic data into a hierarchy of data objects. These data objects are stored in feature classes, object classes, and feature datasets. An object class is a table in the geodatabase that stores nonspatial data.

Geodatabase

Before creating geodatabase, you need to understand following items of geodatabase:

- Spatial reference
- Spatial index grid size
- Field properties
- Field, table, and feature class aliases
- Tracking properties of geometry
- Feature datasets
- Topologies
- Geometric networks
- Relationship classes Spatial reference

1.3.1 Spatial reference

When creating a new feature dataset or standalone feature class, you must specify its spatial reference. The spatial reference for a feature class describes its coordinate system (for example, geographic, UTM, or State Plane), its spatial domain, and its precision. The spatial domain is best described as the allowable coordinate range for x, y coordinates, m- (measure) values, and z- (elevation) values. The precision describes the number of system units per one unit of measure. A spatial reference with a precision of 1 will store integer values and a precision of 1,000 will store three decimal places. Once the spatial reference for a feature dataset or standalone feature class has been set, only the coordinate system can be modified—the spatial domain is fixed.

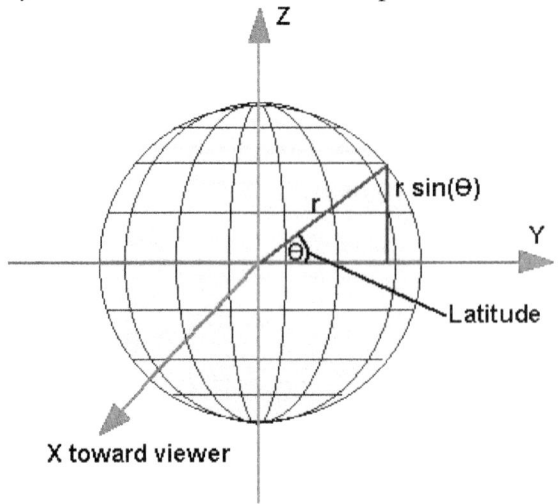

The spatial reference is an important part of geodatabase design because its spatial domain describes the maximum spatial extent to which the data can grow. You must be careful to choose an appropriate x, y, m, and z domain.

1.3.2 Spatial index and grid size

ArcMap uses grids to quickly locate features in feature classes. Identifying a feature, selecting features by pointing or dragging a box, and panning and zooming all require ArcMap to use the spatial index grid to locate features.

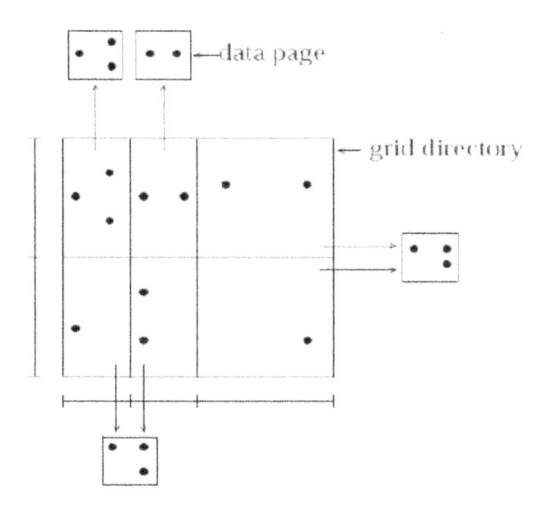

1.3.3 Field properties

When you use ArcCatalog to create a new table or feature class, you can specify any number of fields to be included. You can also specify settings for fields, such as the field type and the maximum size of the data that can be stored in the field.

1.3.4 Default field properties

Use the default value property if you want the field to be

automatically populated with a default value when a new feature or object is created with the ArcMap editing tools. You can set a domain, which is a valid set or range of values that can be stored in the field, by using the domain property.

1.3.5 Field precision and scale

The precision and scale of a field describe the maximum size and precision of data that can be stored in the field. The precision describes the number of digits that can be stored in the field and the scale describes the number of decimal places for and double fields. When creating a new field in a geodatabase feature class or table, you can specify the field's type, precision, and scale. When the field is actually created in the database, the field type may be changed based on the precision and scale values you specify.

1.3.6 Required fields

All tables and feature classes have a set of required fields that are necessary to record the state of any particular object in the table or feature class. These required fields are automatically created when you create a new feature class or table, and they cannot be deleted. Required fields may also have required properties such as their domain property. You cannot modify the required property of a required field.

1.3.7 Field, table, and feature class aliases

The names of feature classes and tables in a geodatabase

are the same as the names of the physical tables in the DBMS in which they are stored. When storing data in a DBMS, often the names for tables and fields are cryptic, and a detailed data dictionary is required to keep track of what data each table stores and what each field in those tables represents.

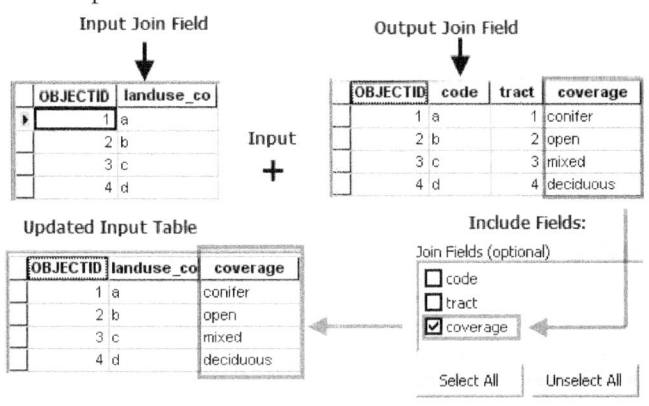

The geodatabase provides the ability to create aliases for fields, tables, and feature classes. An alias is an alternative name to refer to those objects. Unlike true names, aliases do not have to adhere to the limitations of the database, so they can contain special characters such as spaces. In the above example, you may set the alias for the "Pole" table to "Utility Poles", and the alias for the "HGT" field to "Height". In ArcMap, when using data with aliases, the alias name is automatically used for feature classes, tables, and fields. However, in ArcCatalog these objects are always represented by their true names. You can view the alias for feature classes, tables, and fields by examining their properties.

Aliases can be specified when creating a feature class or table and can be modified at any time. Similarly, when creating new fields, the alias is set as a property of that field and can be modified at any time.

1.3.8 Tracking properties of geometry

Often when working with spatial data, you may want to query your data based on properties of the geometry. Line feature classes have a field that tracks the features length, and polygon feature classes have fields that track both the features' area and perimeter. When changes are made to the geometry, the values in these fields are automatically updated. These fields behave like other fields, except that you cannot delete them, assign default values and attribute domains to them, or assign values to them while editing in ArcMap.

1.3.9 Feature datasets

Feature datasets exist in the geodatabase to define a scope for a particular spatial reference. All feature classes that participate in topological relationships with one another (for example, a geometric network or topology) must have the same spatial reference. Feature datasets are a way to group feature classes with the same spatial reference so they can participate in topological relationships with each other.

1.3.10 Topologies

Many vector datasets have features that can share boundaries or corners. If you create a topology in the dataset, you can set up rules defining how features share their geometry. Editing a boundary or vertex shared by two or more features updates the shape of each of those features. Topology rules can govern the relationships between features within a single feature class or between features in two different feature classes. For example, moving a slope boundary in one feature class could update two slope-class polygons and also update the boundary of a forest stand in another feature class.

1.3.11 Geometric networks

Some vector datasets, particularly those used to model communications, material or energy flow, or transportation networks, need to support connectivity tracing and network connectivity rules. Geometric networks allow you to turn simple point and line features into network edge and junction features that can be used for network analysis. Connectivity rules of geometric networks let you control what types of network features may be connected together when editing the network. Geometric networks, like topologies, must be created from a set of feature classes in the same feature dataset.

1.3.12 Relationship classes

Relationship classes define relationships between objects in the geodatabase. These relationships can be simple one-to-one relationships, such as you might create between a feature and a row in a table, or more complex one-to-many (or many-to-many) relationships between features and table rows. Some relationships specify that a given feature, row, or table is not only related to another, but that creating, editing, or deleting one will have a specified effect on the other. These are called composite relationships, and they can be used to ensure that the links between objects in the database are maintained and up-to-date. Deleting a feature, such as a power pole, can trigger the deletion of other features, such as a transformer mounted on the pole, or the maintenance records in a related table.

Area selection is an important process. Based on the work requirement, we choose the area. You have to select an area which have multiple features, so that geodatabase become significant and efficient. Based on the features of geodatabase, later you can analyze data, and then produce output.

In geodatabase, it is compulsory that you should properly place each feature in its proper place. For example while collecting information regarding roads, Road feature data set should be defined in schema and all types of roads should take place under the road feature data set.

Geodatabases organize geographic data into a hierarchy of data objects. These data objects are stored in feature classes, object classes, and feature datasets. An object class is a table in the geodatabase that stores nonspatial data.

ArcCatalog contains tools for creating object classes (tables), feature classes, and feature datasets. Once these items are created in the geodatabase, further items such as subtypes, simple relationship classes, composite relationship classes, geometric networks, and topologies can also be created.

1.4 Practical – Getting Started

1.4.1 Getting started with ArcGIS

1. Open ArcMap from start button of windows.

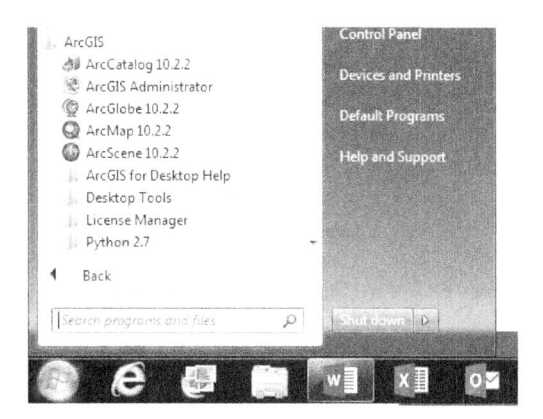

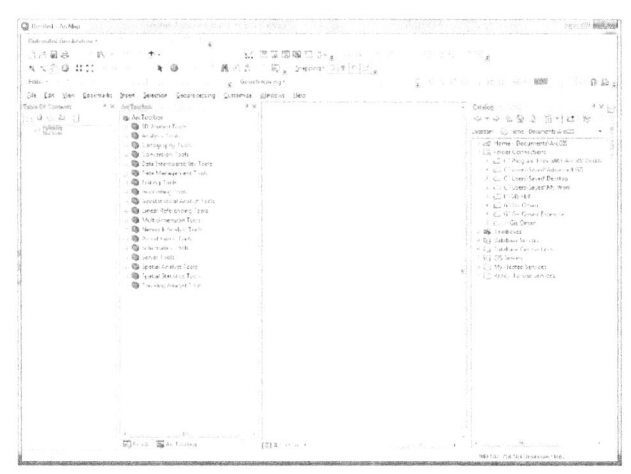

- With the Toolbars tab of the Customize dialog box, existing toolbars can be turned off and on, renamed, or deleted. Any changes can be undone by resetting an individual toolbar to its original state by choosing Reset in the Customize dialog box.

- Also, use the Toolbars tab to create brand new toolbars. When creating a new toolbar, the system will prompt for the new toolbar's name and create a small gray box on the user interface. Add commands to the new toolbar using the Commands tab of the Customize dialog box.

1.4.2 Understands ArcMap

ArcMap is the main component of Esri's ArcGIS suite of geospatial processing programs, and is used primarily to view, edit, create, and analyze geospatial data. ArcMap allows the user to explore data within a data set, symbolize features accordingly, and create maps.

ArcCatalog

ArcCatalog contains tools for creating object classes (tables), feature classes, and feature datasets. Once these items are created in the geodatabase, further items such as subtypes, simple relationship classes, composite relationship classes, geometric networks, and topologies can also be created.
ArcGIS applications include a catalog window that is used to organize and manage various types of geographic information as logical collections—for example, the data, maps, and results of your current GIS project that you work with in ArcGIS. These include the following:

- Geodatabases
- Raster files
- Map documents, globe documents, and layer files
- Geoprocessing toolboxes
- GIS services published using ArcGIS Server
- Standards-based metadata for geographic datasets

The Catalog window provides a tree view of file folders and geodatabases. File folders are used to organize your ArcGIS documents and files. Geodatabases are used to organize your GIS datasets.

ArcToolbox

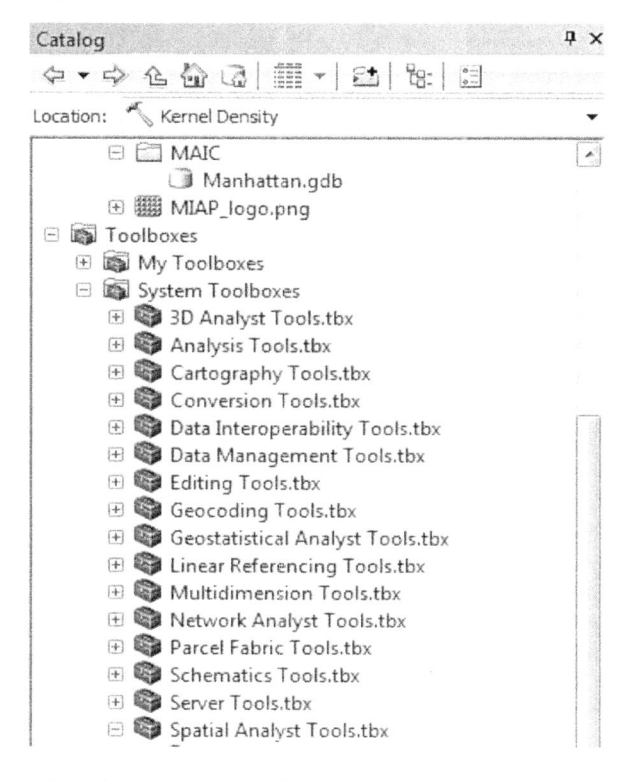

```
Catalog                                          ⇄ ×
⇐ ▾ ⇒ ⌂ ⌂ ⌂ | ▦ ▾ | ⌂ | ⌂ | ⌂
Location:    Kernel Density                        ▾
    ⊟ ▭ MAIC
            ⌗ Manhattan.gdb
      ⊞ ▦ MIAP_logo.png
    ⊟ ▦ Toolboxes
      ⊞ ▦ My Toolboxes
      ⊟ ▦ System Toolboxes
        ⊞ ▦ 3D Analyst Tools.tbx
        ⊞ ▦ Analysis Tools.tbx
        ⊞ ▦ Cartography Tools.tbx
        ⊞ ▦ Conversion Tools.tbx
        ⊞ ▦ Data Interoperability Tools.tbx
        ⊞ ▦ Data Management Tools.tbx
        ⊞ ▦ Editing Tools.tbx
        ⊞ ▦ Geocoding Tools.tbx
        ⊞ ▦ Geostatistical Analyst Tools.tbx
        ⊞ ▦ Linear Referencing Tools.tbx
        ⊞ ▦ Multidimension Tools.tbx
        ⊞ ▦ Network Analyst Tools.tbx
        ⊞ ▦ Parcel Fabric Tools.tbx
        ⊞ ▦ Schematics Tools.tbx
        ⊞ ▦ Server Tools.tbx
        ⊟ ▦ Spatial Analyst Tools.tbx
```

- The ArcToolbox window is dockable in any ArcGIS Desktop application. It provides access to tools you have stored on disk.
- Click the Show/Hide ArcToolbox Window button on the Standard toolbar to open the ArcToolbox window.

- Toolboxes can contain system tools—tools installed by default—or they can contain custom tools that you have created.
- To add a toolbox, right-click the ArcToolbox folder in the ArcToolbox window and click Add Toolbox. Click the Look in dropdown arrow and click the connection to your local copy of the tutorial data

The Commands tab on the Customize dialog box contains all existing ArcMap or ArcCatalog commands. Select a particular command and drag it from the Customize dialog box onto a toolbar as a button or onto a menu as a menu choice. Set a location for saving these customizations—either save customizations in the current map document (.mxd), or in the Normal template (.mxt). Choosing the current .mxd makes the customizations available only for that particular document. Saving customizations to the Normal template makes the customizations available every time a new document is created.

Table of contents Window

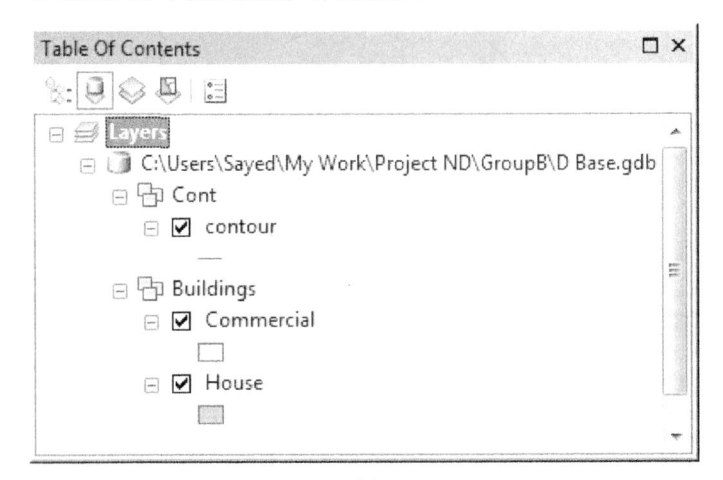

The table of contents lists all the layers on the map and shows what the features in each layer represent. The map's table of contents helps you manage the display order of map layers and symbol assignment, as well as set the display and other properties of each map layer.

The layers at the top of the table of contents draw on top of those below them. Thus, you'll put the layers that form the background of your map, such as the ocean or an image, near the bottom of the table of contents and the layers to which you want to draw the map reader's attention near the top. A typical map might have an image or a terrain base (such as shaded relief or elevation contours) near the bottom. Next, comes base map polygon features, followed by line and point features near the top. And finally, you might typically see some reference layers, such as road names and place-names that provide locational context.

You use the check box or icon to the left of each map layer to turn it on or off. Holding down the CTRL key and clicking turns all map layers on and off simultaneously.

Listing by drawing order

Use List By Drawing Order to author the contents of your map, such as to change the display order of layers on the map, rename or remove layers, and create or manage group layers. All the data frames in your map are listed when the table of contents is sorted by drawing order. However, only the active data frame—indicated by a bold data frame name—is shown in the map in data view.

Listing by source

Click List By Source to show the layers in each data frame

with the layers organized by the folders or databases in which the data sources referenced by the layers can be found. This view will also list tables that have been added to the map document as data.

Listing by visibility

Click List By Visibility to see a dynamic listing of the layers currently displayed in the active data frame. The way layers are listed updates automatically as you pan and zoom, interact with the map, select features, and turn layers on and off.

Listing by selection

Click List By Selection to group layers automatically by whether or not they are selectable and have selected features. A selectable layer means that features in the layer can be selected using the interactive selection tools, such as those on the Tools toolbar or the Edit tool, when in an edit session.

Display options for the table of contents

You can use the Options button on the table of contents to set display properties.

Setting up default geodtabase

1. You can set the path to the default geodatabase in the Getting Started dialog box that appears when you start ArcMap:

MAPPING IN GIS

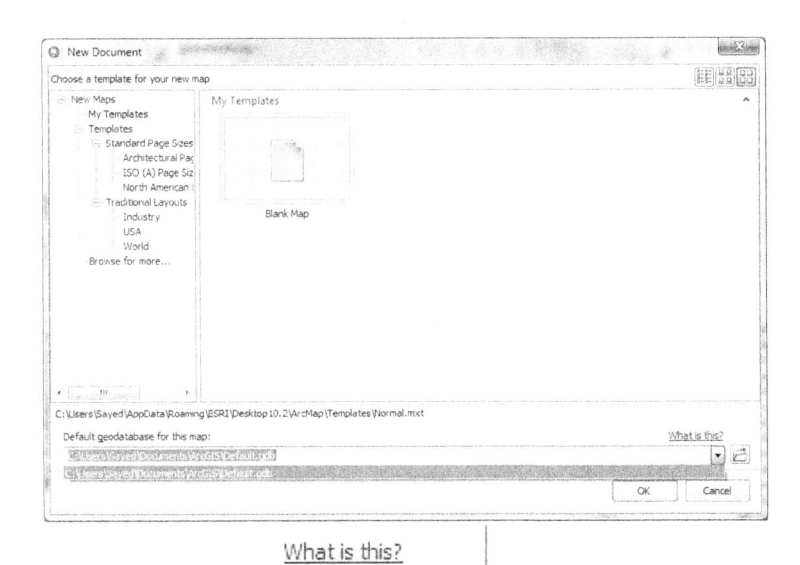

2. Click ▼ 📂 to browse for geodtabase and click add

3. Click ▼ 📂 to browse for geodatabase and click add

MAPPING IN GIS

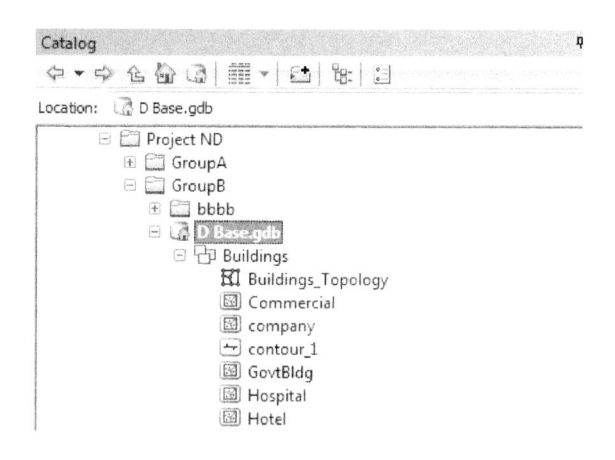

4.

```
Catalog
Location: D Base.gdb
    Project ND
        GroupA
        GroupB
            bbbb
            D Base.gdb
                Buildings
                    Buildings_Topology
                    Commercial
                    company
                    contour_1
                    GovtBldg
                    Hospital
                    Hotel
```

2. Geodatabase Design

2.1 Conceptual Design

During requirement analysis and the conceptual design, Conceptual data models are used in the initial phases of a geodatabase project. Conceptual design is divided into three sub categories:

Input:
- Revised problem statement
- Requirements (ranked)
- Statement of Deliverables

Tasks:
- Establish desired design functions
- Generate conceptual design alternatives
- Compare conceptual design alternatives

Output:
- Most promising conceptual design(s)

In geodatabase design, conceptual design is the first step. We need to go through the following points, these point support us to make project theory:

2.1.1 Identify key information layers

Define more completely some of the key aspects of each data theme. Determine how each dataset will be used—for editing, GIS modelling and analysis, representing your business workflows, and mapping and 3D display. Specify the map use, the data sources, and the spatial representations for each specified map scale; data accuracy and collection guidelines for each map view and 3D view; how the theme is displayed, its symbology, text labels, and annotation. Consider how each map layer will be displayed in an integrated fashion with other key layers. For modelling and analysis, consider how information will be used with other datasets (for example, how they are combined and integrated). This will help you to identify some key spatial relationships and data integrity rules. Ensure that these 2D and 3D map display and analysis properties are considered as part of your database design.

2.1.2 Specify scale ranges and spatial representation:

Data is compiled for use at a specific range of map scales. Associate your geographic representation for each map scale. Geographic representation will often change between map scales (for example, from polygon to line or point). In many cases, you may need to generalize the feature representations for use at smaller scales. Raster can be resampled using image pyramids. In other situations, you may need to collect alternative representations for different map scales.

2.1.3 Group representation into datasets

Your GIS database design should reflect the work of your organization. Consider compiling and maintaining an inventory of map products, analytic models, Web mapping applications, data flows, database reports, key responsibilities, 3D views, and other mission-based requirements for your organization. List the data sources you currently use in this work. Use these to drive your data design needs.

2.2 Logical Design Phase

In this phase, the key task is to exactly define the set

objects of interests and to classify the relationships between them. The objects usually consider as everyday things, such as roads, land, buildings, owners, etc. The relationship is expressed in natural language, such as the "near", "owner", and "behind".

Designing the data model is generally not a direct process. The original model may be filled with data, can be tested, and may be associated to the needs of the user and the user's organization (company, agency, and authority), a business practice or policy. Particularly important to involve to the design the representatives of users group. This is the key to reaching the needs of users by a satisfactory data model. As already mentioned, the creation of logical data model is an iterative process, and are typically based on experiences. Does not exist somewhere in a "real" model, but there are better and less good models.

2.2.1 Define database structure and behavior

It is difficult to determine exactly when the database structure is a good and complete, but there is some indication:

- Is the logical data model contains all the information possible, without repetition?
- Does the logical data model supports the organization's business (legislative) policies?

- Does the logical data model contains the different views of different groups of users for the data?

2.2.2 Define spatial properties

The following table shows the basic elements of the logical data model and their corresponding database elements:

Logical elements	Database elements
feature	row
attribute	field or column
class	table

The logical data model is an abstraction of the feature that we encounter in the specific application. This abstraction is converted to the database elements. The feature represents a real object, such as buildings, lakes or the consumer. The feature is stored as row in the table header. Objects have a set of attribute data. The attribute data shows the quality parameters of the object, such as name, size, quality or identifier as the key to another object. The attributes are stored in columns (or fields) in the database. The class is a collection of similar features. In a class all instances of the same data set descriptor. The class is stored in the database as a table. The rows and columns in a table forms a two –dimensional matrix.

2.3 Physical Design Phase

The physical database is prepared on the basis of the logical database model. In most cases, a skilled professionals for relational database construction will receive the logical data model from the data modeler. By the commands of the database management software, the database manager creates a database structure, and defines the parts of the database. Then you can read or typing in the data. The physical database is very similar to the logical database, but for technical reasons it differs much from it. For display, in the tables the objects can be merged or splitted. The rules and relationships can be expressed in different ways. The main advantage of the geodatabase model, so that the data is included, that they can best recall to the logical data model. In other words, the physical transformation is not completely hiding the database logic from the user. The former (e.g., file-oriented) databases were only available through a programmable interface, the user cannot see anything about the internal structure of the database. The main disadvantage was that the user always had to rely to the developer.

2.3.1 Implement design

The relational database management implements a simple, elegant, easy to understand and transparent structure. The simplicity is also the disadvantage - a relational database is easy to define, but difficult to model complex data. However, the geographic database contain complex data types. The line or a series of closed polygon are structured sets of coordinates, and cannot be described as an elementary data type like integer, floating number or string. In addition, the features have collected in a database, should include topological information and spatial relations and overall relationship as well. A relational database is the foundation for the geodatabase. The main purpose of the geodatabase is to handle complex data in unified data model, independent of the relational database management underneath.

2.3.2 Design building and maintaining work flows

The structure of geodatabase lets you design geographic datasets that are close to their logical data model.

These are the basic steps in designing a geodatabase:

- Modelling the user's view. Perform talk (interview) with users, understand organization, and analyze the current and possibly future needs of users.
- The definition of objects and their relationships. The objects should be incorporated into the logical data model to take account of how relations are between them.
- Select the geographic representation. We need to decide whether a vector, raster, or the surface is best to represent the data of interest.
- Match to elements of the geodatabase. Fit the objects in the logical data model into the elements of a geodatabase.
- Organize geodatabase structure. Build the structure of a geodatabase. Consider thematic groupings, topological associations and department responsibility of data.

2.3.3 Document your design

A concise and understandable form for documentation of this stage the design is to preparation simple UML diagram. The following illustration shows a UML diagram of an example:

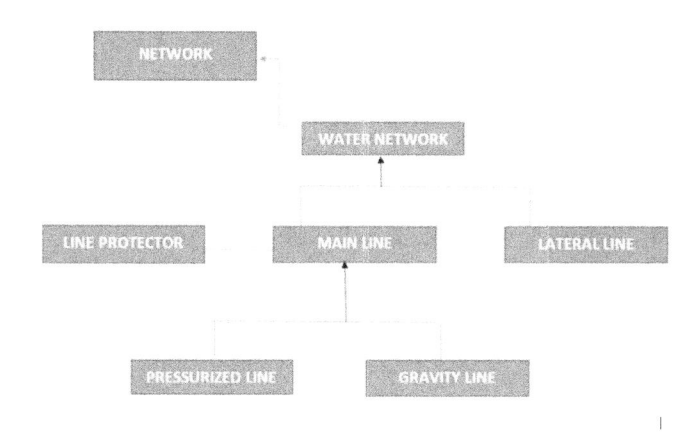

```
                    NETWORK
                       |
                 WATER NETWORK
                       ↑
      ┌────────────────┼────────────────┐
 LINE PROTECTOR     MAIN LINE       LATERAL LINE
                       ↑
              ┌────────┴────────┐
        PRESSURIZED LINE    GRAVITY LINE
```

The above diagram states the following:

- A water line is a type of network line,
- A main line and a lateral line make up a type of water line,
- A main line can be associated with zero to many line protectors,
- A pressurized and gravity main are types of main lines.

The steps created so far can be summarized in the following table:

Entity	Relation
Water utility	
pump	-
water meter	-
meter box	water meter
valve	-
main line	--
treatment plant	-
Land title	
parcel	-
easement	-
parcel record	parcel
parcel image	-
owner	parcel
address of owner	-
Street network	
street	-
bridge	-
street name	street
traffic light	-

bus route	-
bus stop	-
Environment	
monument	-
fence	-
vegetation	-
place names	-
river valley	-
satellite image	

2.4 Things to be consider before designing geodatabase

The following rules will help in the choice of representation. The information developed in this step should be summarized in a data dictionary. This dictionary is intended to document the appearance of individuals in the geodatabase.

- **Point** – for a feature whose is too small to be defined as area in a database of a given resolution
- **Line** – for a feature whose is too narrow to be defined as area in a database of a given resolution
- **Area** – illustrates the location and polygonal shape of a feature on a map of a given scale
- **Surface** – illustrates the shape as in an area, but shows the shape resulting from changes in elevation

- **Raster** – represent features as an area of rectangular cells
- **Image, photo, drawing** – each represent a digital picture and cannot be used for spatial analysis
- **Object (or Binary Large Object)** – identifies a feature which are not like above, and not have geometric representation (video, voice, office document, web page)

3. Software Analyses Tools for GIS

3.1 Introduction

You have been introduced to geospatial data types, its sources, data products and formats in previous units. You have learnt that geospatial data has both spatial and non-spatial information. Handling of any geospatial data requires special tools because of their spatial and non-spatial information contents. Besides the analysis functionalities, the geospatial data handling tools should have the capabilities to create and store data, locate them with geographic location, create outputs and visualize them. In this unit, you will study in detail about the geospatial data analysis tools, their types and comparison. You will also learn about the pointers which would guide you to choose a tool for your study.

3.2 Geospatial Tools

Geospatial tools (or geoinformatics software) are increasingly being used as the principal tools for digital exploration of variation in landscapes, as they provide the necessary functions for spatial data collection, management, analysis and representation. Any geospatial data analysis tool should be capable of generating thematic maps, and allowing overlay of different layers of-information. It should carry out specific calculations, databases linking and also processing satellite images as well as aerial photographs. The recent advances in remote sensing have made it possible to have latest information about the earth at different spatial resolutions, rather than extracting the same information from maps which have been prepared using various symbols and colors.

Geospatial data handling tools form the basis of the processing engine, and comprise a vital component of operational software. Geospatial tools (/software) comprise an integrated collection of computer programs that implement geographic storage, processing and display functions. Geospatial tools' functionality includes the following aspects:

- Allow studying of data, methods and algorithm implementation
- Developed models and algorithms need not be implemented by others in order to continue research or validate previous results
- Ensure worldwide development, advancement and applications.

Apart from these, researchers should have access to libraries of the original models for analysis, validation, development and implementation for further improvement and customization, depending on the local requirement.

A modern geospatial tool, particularly, the GIS comprises an integrated suite of software components of three basic types:

- Data management system for controlling access to data mapping system for display
- Interaction with maps and other geographic visualization, and a spatial
- Analysis and modelling system.

Widely used GIS are built and released by GIS software development and product teams that may operate according to commercial or open-source models. Mature software products are carefully planned versioned release cycles that incrementally enhance and extend the pool of capabilities. The key parts of GIS are:

- architecture - the user interface
- business logic (tools)
- data manager
- data model and
- Customization environment.

GIS product teams start with a formal design of a software system followed by building each part or component separately before assembling the whole system. Mostly the development will be repetitive with creation of an initial prototype framework containing a small number of partially functioning parts' A key choice that is faced by all software developers is whether to design a software system by buying in components, or to build it from scratch' Both options have their own advantages; building components give greater control over system capabilities and enable specific-purpose optimization, whereas buying components can save time and money.

3.3 Advantages of GIS tool

The advantages of geoinformation technologies are encountered through the tasks that the various packages can perform. Specific advantages of geospatial tools are the followings:

- It allows you to map the location of objects, like natural, cultural and human resources. Terrain models can be generated to aid with 3-D visualization. Densities and quantities of a specific item in a given area can be calculated and displayed, as can population changes over time
- It helps you to know specific street address and coordinate data (i.e. longitudes and latitudes) which can be accurately computed from a map using geocoding methods. The software provides a very

effective means for graphically conveying the complex information
- It can help you organize and centralize your data. A GIS database can link all of your organization's digital data together based on locations, such as addresses. This could enable all departments of an organization to have access to, and share the same data, and ensure all departments and individuals are using the most up-to-date information.
- Websites can be developed with geoinformatics software for either the internet or company intranet applications which can help your company or organization to effectively convey information to members of p private group, or public at large. Maps can be created dynamically and uploaded over the web.
- Field based GPS data can be analyzed, displayed and plotted, and subsequently imported into your organization's database using geospatial tools.

3.4 Commercial off the Shelf (COTS)

Commercial off-The-shelf (COTS) software is considered an economically viable method of integrating various software components to produce a new product. Many commercial and government organizations are now relying on COTS software rather than developing and maintaining their own programs. COTS products seem to be less expensive than the proprietary software to integrate into the infrastructure of an organization, whilst decreasing the development time for new products. COTS software products have been defined as "commercial items that have been sold, leased, or licensed in a quantity of at least 10 copies in the commercial marketplace, at an advertised price"

(National Research Council, 1997). COTS software products include a description or definition of the functions the software performs, documented to good commercial standards, and a definition of the resources needed to run the software. Four issues need to be considered when considering COTS software:

- functionality and performance,
- interoperability,
- Product evolution. and
- Vendor behavior.

There are gamut of COTS software available in the market, which include PCI Geomatica, ERDAS Imagine, ENVI, ArcGIS, MapInfo, IDRSI, etc. we take ESRI- Arc GIS and ERDAS Imagine, as two examples of COTS.

3.4.1 ArcGIS

ArcMap is the main component of ESRI's ArcGIS suite of geospatial processing programs, and is used primarily to view, edit, create, and analyses geospatial data. ArcMap allows the user to explore data within a data set, symbolize features accordingly, and create maps.

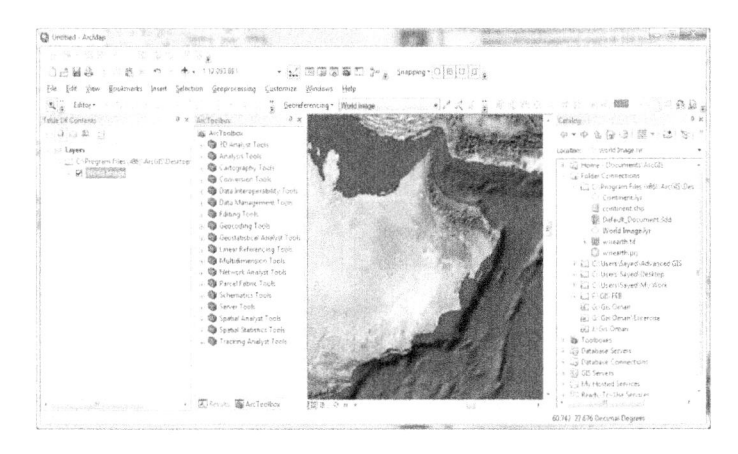

ArcMap users can create and manipulate data sets to include a variety of information. For example, the maps produced in ArcMap generally include features, such as north arrow, scale bars, titles, legends, etc. The software package includes a style-set of these features.

The ArcGIS suite is available at three license levels: ArcEditor (Basic), ArcView (Standard) and Arclnfo (Advanced). Each step up in the license provides the user with more extensions that allow a variety 'of querying to be performed on a data set' Maps created and saved within will create a file on the hard drive with an .mxd extension. Once the .mxd file is opened in ArcMap, the user can display a variety of information, as long as it exists within the data set. At this time, the user will create an entirely new map output and use the customization and design features to create a unique product. Upon completion of the map, ArcMap has the ability to save, print, and export files to .Pdf.

3.4.2 ERDAS IMAGTNE

ERDAS IMAGINE is a geoinformatics application tool with raster graphics editor capabilities designed by ERDAS Inc. for geospatial application. It is aimed primarily at geospatial raster data processing and allows the user to prepare, display and enhance digital images for mapping use in GIS or in-CADD software. It is a toolbox allowing the user to perform numerous operation on an image and generates an answer to specific geographical questions. By manipulating imagery data values and positions, it is possible to see features that would not normally be visible and to locate geo- positions of features that would otherwise be graphical. The level of brightness or reflectance of light from the surfaces in the image can be helpful for vegetation analysis, prospecting minerals, etc. other usage examples include linear feature extraction, generation of processing work flows (spatial models in ERDAS IMAGINE), import/export of data for a wide variety of formats, ortho rectification, mosaicking of imagery, stereo and automatic feature extraction of thematic map data from imagery.

3.4.3 Envi

ENVI, which is an acronym for "Environment for Visualizing Images", is a software application used to process and analyses geospatial imagery. It is marketed by ITT Visual information Solutions, and is commonly used by remote sensing professionals, scientists, researchers, and image analysts. ENVI software provides scientifically advanced image processing and analysis capabilities accessible to all levels of geospatial imagery users. The software uses an automated, wizard-based approach that walks users through complex tasks. ENVI was originally developed by adapting the U. S. Geological Survey's REMAPP-PC public domain, and was subsequently sold to Kodak.

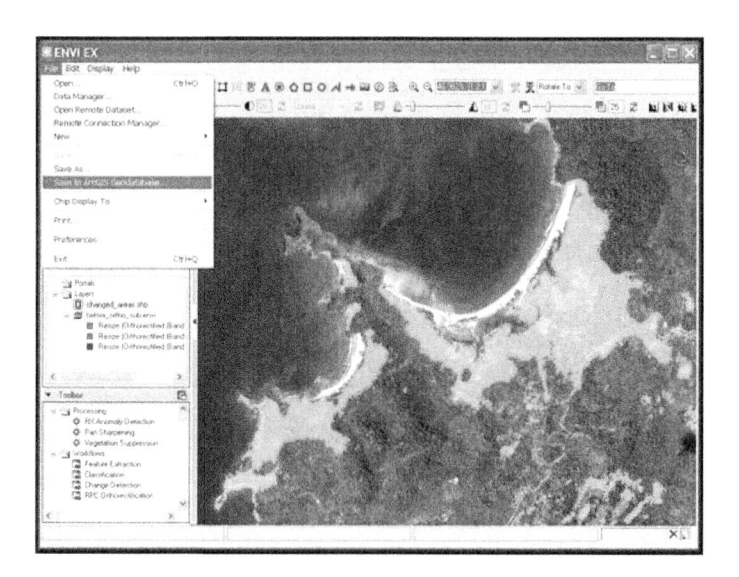

3.5 Free hand open source software (FOSS)

You will find it interesting to read and understand about the open source software - FLOSS. This kind of software is generally distributed along with its source code. This is usually done free with the purpose of allowing the improvement of the software by the general user and developer base. This way, the software can definitely apply to user needs and interests as well as draw closer to perfection in the most efficient way possible. Many organizations have adopted the open source philosophy in order to produce the premier software of their markets, and many non-profit organizations have coalesced in support of open source software. Even governments have heralded their support of open source Software, and some have even gone as far as to initiate mandates that render the distribution of open source software all but compulsory.

3.5.1 Usage and functionality

The uses of FOSS are many besides being cheap. Some of the uses of FOSS are listed below:

- Marketable skills: In this ever-changing job market, it is a huge benefit to be able to bring a total software package to the table.
- Supported by huge development and support community: FOSS community is very passionate about helping each other and continually improving software.
- Low start-up costs: It is now possible to install a complete GIS stack without paying any thing legally.
- Security: Arguably more secure than proprietary software backed by a large development community. Increasingly, now-a-days, bugs are found and filed quickly.
- Workability: It works on all major platforms, like Mac, Linux, Windows.
- Works with existing Grs data: import .shp files, most major formats, and export to most major formats. ArcSDE now connects to postGIS (os database)p, and above all there is no file format lock-in.

3.5.2 Examples
3.5.2.1 Grass GIS

Geographic Resources Analysis Support System' commonly referred to as GRASS, is a free GIS software used for geospatial data management and analysis, image processing, graphics/mafs production, spatial modelling and visualization. GRASS is used in many academic and commercial settings around the world, as well as by many government agencies, including NASA, NOAA, USDA, DLR, CSIRO, the National Park Service, the U.S.Census Bureau,USGS,and many environmental consulting companies. GRASS is an official project of the Open Source Geospatial Foundation.

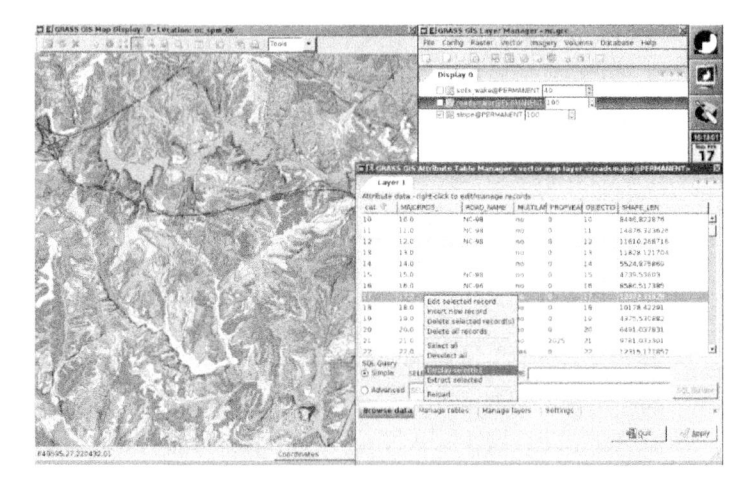

3.5.2.2 Quantum GIS

Quantum GIS (QGIS) is a user friendly open Source GIS licensed under the GNU (General Public License). QGIS is an official project of the open Source Geospatial Foundation (OSGeo). It is a multi-platform application and runs on different operating systems such as Linux, UNIX, Mac OSX and Windows and supports numerous vector, raster, and database formats and functionalities. Quantum GIS provides a continuously growing number of capabilities provided by core functions and plug-ins. You can visualize, manage, edit, analyses data, and compose printable maps. You will get a first impression of the software with the screenshot in Fig.7.5. QGIS is a cross-platform (Linux, windows, Mac) open source application with many common GIS features and functions.

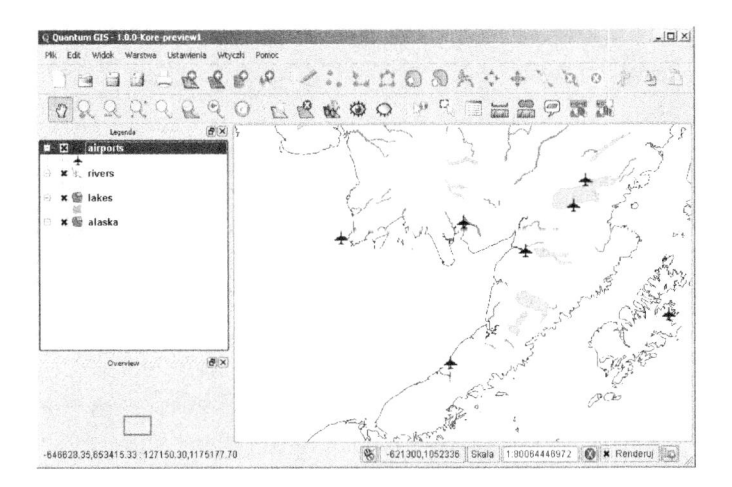

3.6 Hardware requirements and constraints

There are certain basic requirements for installing the geoinformatics software. The ever-growing development and innovation in the field of computer hardware and software industry generally require continuous updation and upgradation of both software and hardware. It is neither possible nor desirable to recommend a generalised requirement in terms of hardware and software for a GIS program. It is obvious that hardware and software requirements vary considerably depending on the tasks trndertaken. The following minimum configuration allows installation of most modern GIS applications for work with small components:

- 2.8 Ghz PIV true PC compatible (dual-core processor recommended).
- 1 GB RAM (4 GB or greater recommended).

- 800 x 600 SVGA Display (1280 x 1024 or greater recommended).
- 250 MB hard disk free space (gigabytes of free space recommended).
- Windows 2000, Windows XP, Windows Server 2003, Windows Server 2008 or Vista with most recent service pack, in standard 32-bit versions or in 64-bit versions. (Windows XP or greater recommended).
- Internet Explorer 6 or most recent IE version plus most recent service pack.
- Microsoft's .NET Framework 2.0 or more recent.
- IIS 5.1 or greater to operate IMS.

4.1 DBMS (Database Management System)

Since the early '90, Geographical Information System (GIS) has become a classy system for maintaining and analyzing spatial and thematic information on spatial objects. DBMSs are progressively important in GIS, since DBMSs are usually used to handle large volumes of data and to guarantee the logical consistency and integrity of data, which also have become major requirements in GIS. Today spatial data is mostly part of a whole work and information process. In many organizations there is a need to implement GIS functionality as part of a central Database Management System (DBMS), at least at the abstract level, in which spatial data and alphanumerical data are maintained in one integrated environment. Consequently DBMS occupies a central place in the new generation GIS architecture.

A DBMS contains:
- Data definition language
- Data dictionary
- Data-entry module
- Data update module
- Report generator
- Query language

4.1 Data definition language

Data definition language or data description language (DDL) used to build and modify the organization of your tables and other objects in the database. DDL defines your database.

4.2 Data dictionary

A data dictionary is a collection of descriptions of the data objects in a data model for the benefit of users and others who need to refer to them. It describes each item's type and size that occupied by datatype. In database management systems, a file that defines the basic organization of a database. Most database management systems keep the data dictionary hidden from users to prevent them from accidentally destroying its contents.

4.3 Data-entry module

Data is entered manually through a data entry interface specified by the user through a worksheet definition. Normally data entry provided by DBMS software

4.4 Data update model

The module which provide facility to update entered data. Using this module, one can update existing data according to current requirement.

4.5 Report generator

Report generator is a tool whose purpose is to take data from a source such as a database, XML stream or a spreadsheet, and use it to produce a document in a format which satisfies a particular human readership.

4.6 Query language

Query language are used to make queries in database. To analyze something from database, we need to perform query. In a large database query is essential feature, without query one cannot get results instantly.

4.7 Architecture of DBMS:

The design of a DBMS depends on its architecture. It can be centralized or decentralized or hierarchical. The architecture of a DBMS can be seen as either single tier or multi-tier. An n-tier architecture divides the whole system into related but independent n modules, which can be independently modified, altered, changed, or replaced.

4.7.1 – Tier Architecture: In 1-tier architecture, the DBMS is the only entity where the user directly sits on the DBMS and uses it. Any changes done here will directly be done on the DBMS itself. It does not provide handy tools for end-users. Database designers and programmers normally prefer to use single-tier architecture.

4.7.2 – Tier Architecture: If the architecture of DBMS is 2-tier, then it must have an application through which the DBMS can be accessed. Programmers use 2-tier architecture where they access the DBMS by means of an application. Here the application tier is entirely independent of the database in terms of operation, design, and programming.

4.7.3 – Tier Architecture

A 3-tier architecture separates its tiers from each other based on the complexity of the users and how they use the data present in the database. It is the most widely used architecture to design a DBMS.

Database (Data) Tier – at this tier, the database resides along with its query processing languages. We also have the relations that define the data and their constraints at this level.

Application (Middle) Tier – at this tier reside the application server and the programs that access the database. For a user, this application tier presents an abstracted view of the database. End-users are unaware of any existence of the database beyond the application. At the other end, the database tier is not aware of any other user beyond the application tier. Hence, the application layer sits in the middle and acts as a mediator between the end-user and the database.

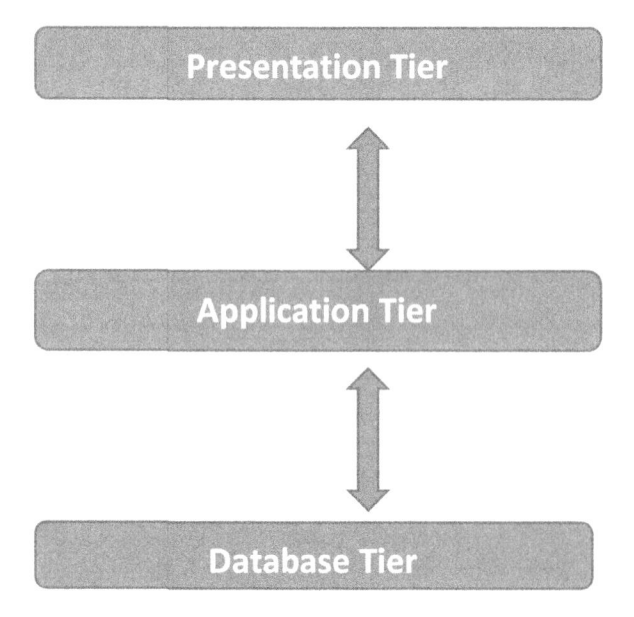

Presentation Tier

⇕

Application Tier

⇕

Database Tier

User (Presentation) Tier – End-users operate on this tier and they know nothing about any existence of the database beyond this layer. At this layer, multiple views of the database can be provided by the application. All views are generated by applications that reside in the application tier.

Multiple-tier database architecture is highly modifiable, as almost all its components are independent and can be changed independently.

4.9 Database models

Every database must follow to the principles of some data model. However, the term data model is somewhat confusing. A database model is a type of data model that determines the logical structure of a database. A model for database also determines in which manner data can be stored, organized, and manipulated. It is the way of describing and manipulating the data in data base. There are three data models generally used to organize the digital data bases.

4.8.1 Hierarchical Data Model

In this, data are organized in a tree like structure. I.e. root-parent-children. The top hierarchy is termed as a root which is comprised of single entity. It is represented by a single data field or by a record having many data fields. Except for the root every element has one higher level element. Related to it called parent and one more subordinate element termed as children. An element can have only one parent but can have multiple children. An element can have only one parent but can have multiple children. In hierarchical data model every relation is a many-to–one relation or one–to-one relation.

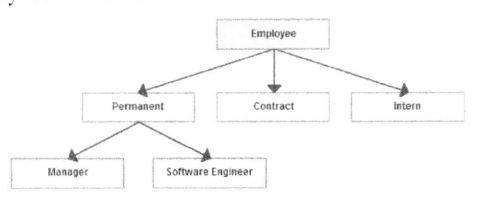

4.8.2 Relational data model

(RDBMS - relational database management system) A database based on the relational model developed by E.F. Codd. A relational database allows the definition of data structures, storage and retrieval operations and integrity constraints. In such a database the data and relations between them are organized in tables. A table is a collection of records and each record in a table contains the same fields.

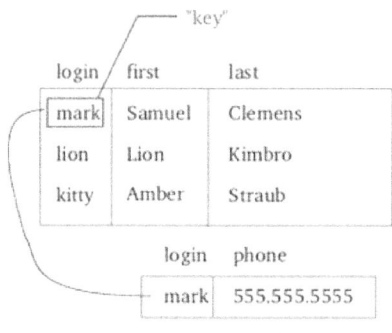

login	first	last
mark	Samuel	Clemens
lion	Lion	Kimbro
kitty	Amber	Straub

login	phone
mark	555.555.5555

"related table"

The main advantages of Relational data model is to perform queries, import export data, and updating/deletion of records.

4.8.3 Network Model

The network data model was created to represent complex relationship between entities. The network model two different data structures to represent the database entities and relationships between the entities, namely record type and set type.

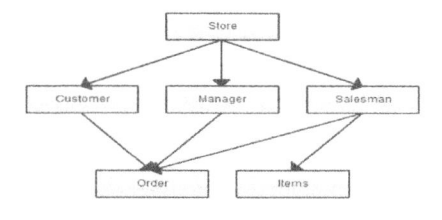

Data Flow Diagrams

Data Flow Diagrams (DFD) can be used to graphically illustrate the flow of data through a system or model. More generically, Flow Diagrams (or Process Flow Diagrams) can be used to depict the movement and process steps of data, information, people, money, electricity, etc. through a system. The basic concept is a means of showing what goes in (to a system or model), what processes occur (within the system or model) and what comes out.

A flow diagram is a graphical means of presenting, describing, or analyzing a process. This is done by drawing small boxes which represent steps or decisions in a chain of steps or decisions. These boxes are connected to other boxes by lines and arrows which represent sequence and dependency relationships (i.e., X must be done before Y can be done).

A DFD for a GIS model or process should include (at a minimum) all of the necessary information for you (or someone else) to recreate the entire sequence of steps used to arrive at a conclusion or data output. This would include:

- Names of input data
- Names of process steps (clip, buffer, overlay, select by attribute)
- Parameters used (.5 mile buffer, Name = New York, etc)
- Names given to data layers generated (big_streets, school_buff)
- Arrows connecting the data (boxes) with the process steps (ovals) indicating the direction

(flow) of data and the order of processing steps

In addition, a DFD should include (either as annotation or footnotes):
- A name or title for the entire process
- Optionally an abstract or summary of the goal
- Source(s) of input data (where you got it, where its stored)
- Final results

Different flow diagrams (charts) use different symbology (shapes of boxes, colors of lines, etc) to communicate, but the principals are fairly similar.

The following symbols are commonly used in many Data Flow Diagrams:
- Input Data (Information sources) are represented by square boxes.
- Processes are represented by labeled ovals (bubbles).
- Output Data are represented by rectangular boxes.
- Data flows (connections) are represented by a labeled arrow.
- Process parameters can be annotated on the flow diagram or footnoted.

However The ModelBuilder in ArcGIS swaps the rectangles and ovals
- Input Data (Information sources) are represented by dark blue ovals.
- Processes are represented by labeled yellow rectangles.
- Output Data are represented by green ovals.

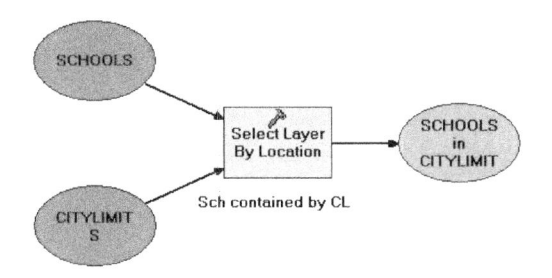

- Data flows (connectors) are represented by a labeled arrow.
- Process parameters can be annotated on the flow diagram or footnoted.

4.10 Practical
4.10.1 Creating database in MS Access

Microsoft Access is a Relational Database Management System (RDBMS), designed primarily for home or small business usage.

Access has traditionally been known as a desktop database system because its functions are intended to be run from a single computer (as opposed to a server database application where the application is installed on a server, then accessed remotely from multiple client machines).

With database management systems, you need to create your tables before you can enter data. Microsoft Access makes creating tables extremely easy. In fact, when you create a database, Access creates your first table for you (and calls it Table1).

4.10.2 Create a table

Normally when you need to create a new table, you'll select CREATE > Table from the Ribbon toolbar. But we can do that later.

For now Access has already created our first table, so all we need to do is modify that table so that it suits our needs.

Using our blank database, we are going to rename Table1 to Customers. This table will have 4 columns: CustomerId, FirstName, LastName, and DateCreated.

Rename the ID field to CustomerId. To do this, Right-click on the ID column and select Rename Field. Enter CustomerId when prompted:

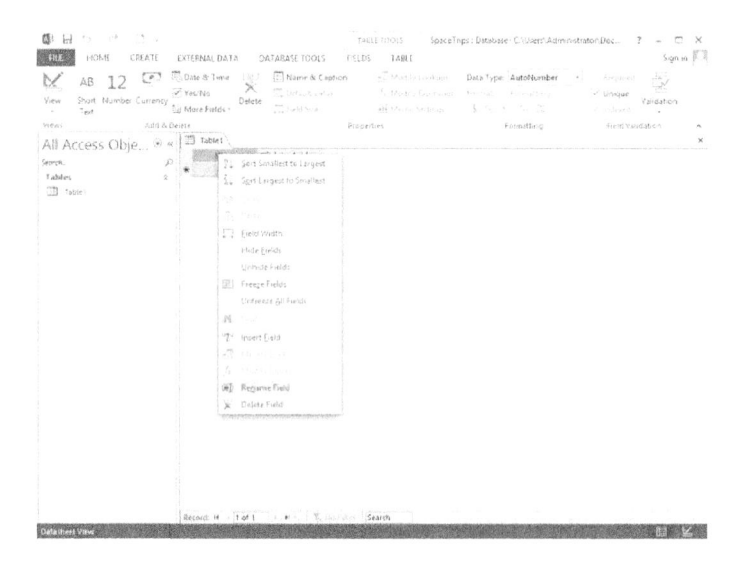

On the next field, click on Click to Add (unless Access has already opened the menu for you) and select Short Text:

At this point, Access will conveniently highlight/select the field name (currently Field1) so that you can name the field. Call it FirstName:

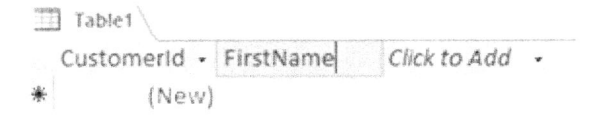

> Do the same again for the next field (LastName) and select data type Short Text.

In the next field, select the Date & Time data type and name the field DateCreated

What we just did was create the column names and specify the type of data that can be entered into them. Restricting the data type for each column is very important and helps maintain data integrity. It can ensure that the user enters the data in the intended format. It can also guard against accidents like for example, inadvertently entering an email address into a field for storing the current date.

Your database table should now look like this:

You might notice that now when you click on the field names, you can't see or change their data types. Instead, if you click on the inverted triangle within a field, you see a different menu of options (eg, Sort Oldest to Newest etc) depending on the field's data type. This shows that the field is ready for data - once you have data, you can sort it using this menu.

Don't worry if you accidentally entered the wrong data type. You can change the dataype in the Ribbon toolbar by adjusting the data type under the Data Type dropdown (top right area of the toolbar). If you can't see this option in the toolbar be sure to select the FIELDS tab first:

We have just created a database table. We did this in Datasheet view.

4.10.3 Export access database to MS Excel

Most Access users will, at some point, need to export their Access database to an Excel spreadsheet. OK, most users don't need to export the whole Access database - they will usually only need to export a table or the results of a query to Excel. Once in Excel, they can use the data as they would normally use data in Excel.

Excel isn't the only format that you might want to export data to. You might want to export from Access to XML, HTML, CSV file, or even a PDF file. Fortunately you can do all of these in Access 2013.

Here's how you export data from MS Access to Excel.

1. Open the table or query that contains the data you want to export
2. Ensuring the EXTERNAL DATA tab is selected on the Ribbon, click the Excel download icon (this is the one with the downward facing arrow):

3. Click OK to save the file at the default location. Alternatively, change the location and/or a file name. You can also select any other options you wish to include:

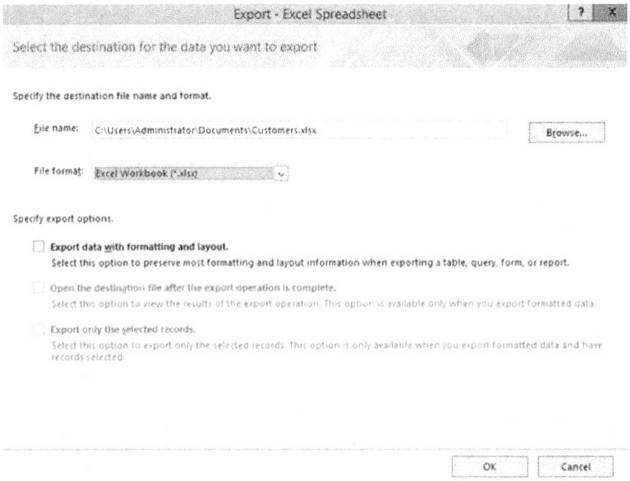

4. Click Close. Alternatively, you could select Save Export Steps before clicking Close.
5. You now have an Excel spreadsheet containing the data from your query that you can send to anyone you like.

5 Geodatabase

5.1 What is geodatabase and spatial data?

A geodatabase is a database that stores related feature (raster and vector) objects. These objects may be point feature, line feature or polyline feature. We can attach raster objects (such as jpg, tiff, and img) to our geodatabase.

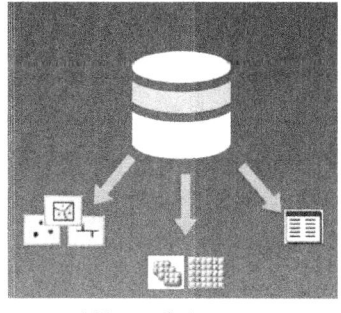

5.2 Spatial data

Spatial data records the relationship among and about geographically distinguishable features. Examples include the location of a rain gauge, area submerged under flood, the route a delivery truck takes, the extent of damage from a forest fire or a tourist place. Like other kinds of data, spatial data can be categorized into primary and secondary spatial data. Representation of real world features as discrete objects is done through two modes of data representation, which embody the linkage between the real world domain of geographic data and computer representation of these features.

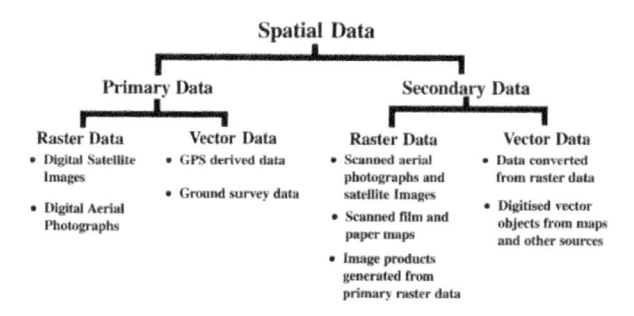

```
                        Spatial Data
              ┌───────────────┴───────────────┐
          Primary Data                   Secondary Data
         ┌──────┴──────┐               ┌──────┴──────┐
    Raster Data   Vector Data     Raster Data    Vector Data
  • Digital Satellite  • GPS derived data   • Scanned aerial      • Data converted
    Images                                    photographs and       from raster data
                       • Ground survey data   satellite Images
  • Digital Aerial                                                 • Digitised vector
    Photographs                             • Scanned film and       objects from maps
                                              paper maps             and other sources

                                            • Image products
                                              generated from
                                              primary raster data
```

Thus, the spatial data fall into two basic categories:

- Vector data represents discrete features, such as customer locations, streets, parcels, land usage an data summarized by area.
  - Raster data represents continuous numeric values, such as elevation, and continuous categories, such as vegetation types, and water.

5.3 Why to use geodatabase

Here are some reasons to use geodatabase

- **Improved versatility and usability:** A geodatabase is like system file, which store binary data and manage geospatial data. Geodatabase can be access by ArcGIS. This provide a simple model for working with information in tables.
- **Optimized performance:** Geodatabase is optimized for performance and storage. Individual feature can be as large as 1TB in size but still provide fast performance.
- **Few size limitations:** Geodatabase size is limited only by available disk space. With the use of configuration keyword, this can be expanded to 1 TB to 256 TB

- **Easy data migration:** Geodatabase support migration also i.e.MDB can be converted to GDB
- **Improved editing model:** Geodatabase support a single data editor and many data viewers concurrently. If a feature class in a feature dataset is being edited, all feature class in that feature dataset are unavailable for editing, but features may still viewed and selected by ArcMap.
- **Storing raster in the geodatabase:** managed raster data is subdivided into small, manageable areas called, tiles, stored as a binary large objects (BLOBs) in the database.
- **Customizable storage**: when creating a dataset, apply optional configuration keywords to customize storage for a particular type of data to improve storage efficiency and performance.
- **Allows updates to spatial index settings:** Spatial indexes are used to quickly locate features when you display, edit or query data. ArcGIS automatically rebuilds the spatial index at the end of some update operations to ensure the index and is grid sizes are optimal.
- **Allows the use of data compression:** Vector data can be stored in a Geodatabase in a compressed, read only format that reduces storage requirements.

5.4 What is the geodatabase?

An ArcGIS geodatabase is a collection of geographic datasets of various types held in a common file system folder, a Microsoft Access database, or a multiuser relational database (such as Oracle, Microsoft SQL Server, or IBM DB2). A key geodatabase concept is the dataset. It is the primary mechanism used to organize and use geographic information in ArcGIS. The geodatabase contains three primary dataset types:

- Feature classes
- Raster datasets
- Tables

Creating a collection of these dataset types is the first step in designing and building a geodatabase. Users typically start by building a number of these fundamental dataset types. Then they add to or extend their geodatabase with more advanced capabilities (such as by adding topologies, networks, or subtypes) to model GIS behavior, maintain data integrity, and work with an important set of spatial relationships.

5.5 Types of geodatabase
5.5.1 File

A collection of various types of GIS datasets held in a file system folder. This is the recommended native data format for ArcGIS stored and managed in a file system folder. File geodatabase are useful for Single user and small workgroups. File geodatabase provides many readers or one writer per feature dataset, stand-alone feature class, or table.

5.5.2 Personal

Original data format for ArcGIS geodatabases stored and managed in Microsoft Access data files. This is limited in size and tied to the Windows operating system. Personal geodatabase provides single user and small workgroups with smaller datasets. Some readers and one writer.

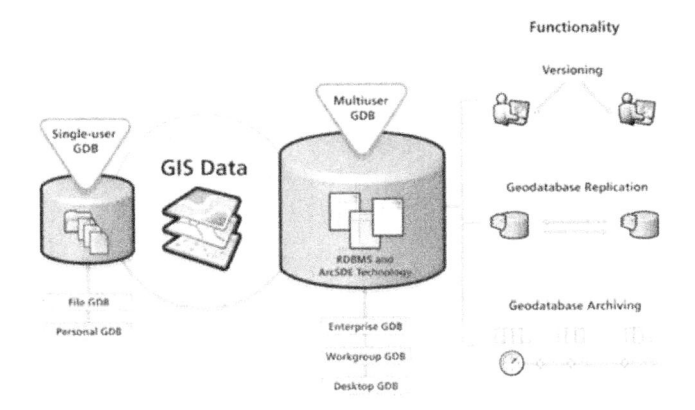

5.5.3 Multiuser geodatabase

A collection of various types of GIS datasets held as tables in a relational database. The recommended native data format for ArcGIS stored and managed in a relational database. Multiuser geodatabase provides Multiuser, Many readers and many writers.

5.6 Architecture of geodatabase

Basic operation of Geodatabase is to physically store the geographic information using some underlying
DBMS or file system. But in addition to physical storage of geographic information Geodatabases has some key aspects.

5.6.1 Information Model

This model is used for representing and managing geographic information. This model is based on a collection of data tables with different geographic datasets (feature class, raster class and attributes).

5.6.2 The application layer

Logic is to access and working with geographic data with different files and formats.

5.6.3 Transaction model

to manage the GIS data flow in the GIS system

5.7 Components of geodatabase
5.7.1 Raster

Raster datasets represent geographic features by dividing the world into discrete square or rectangular cells laid out in a grid. Each cell has a value that is used to represent some characteristic of that location.

5.7.2 Vector

In the vector data, spatial locations of features are defined on the basis of coordinate pairs. In this data format, real world features are represented in the form of lines, points, and polygons.

5.7.3 Coverages

A coverage is a geo relational data model that stores vector data—it contains both the spatial (location) and attribute (descriptive) data for geographic features. Coverages use a set of feature classes to represent geographic features. Each feature class stores a set of points, lines (arcs), polygons, or annotation (text). Coverages can have topology, which determines the relationships between features.

5.7.4 Terrain

A terrain dataset is a multiresolution, TIN-based surface built from measurements stored as features in a geodatabase. They're typically made from LIDAR, sonar, and photogrammetric sources. Terrains reside in the geodatabase, inside feature datasets with the features used to construct them.

5.7.5 Annotation

Annotation in the geodatabase is stored in annotation feature classes. As with other feature classes, all features in an annotation feature class have a geographic location and attributes and can either be inside a feature dataset or a stand-alone feature class. Each text annotation feature has symbology including font, size, color, and any other text symbol property. Annotation is typically text, but it can also include graphic shapes—for example, boxes or arrows—that require other types of symbology.

5.8 Structure of geodatabase

A geodatabase has three primary components—feature classes, feature datasets, and nonspatial tables. All three components are created and managed in ArcCatalog.

- A feature class is a collection of features that share the same geometry type (point, line, or polygon) and spatial reference.
- A feature dataset is a collection of feature classes. All the feature classes in a feature dataset must have the same spatial reference.
- A nonspatial table contains attribute data that can be associated with feature classes.

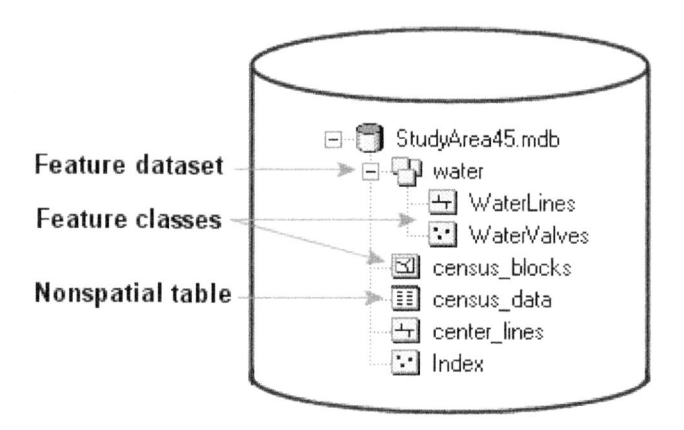

```
                    ┌─ StudyArea45.mdb
Feature dataset ──→ ├─ water
Feature classes ──→ │    ├─ WaterLines
                    │    └─ WaterValves
                    ├─ census_blocks
Nonspatial table ─→ ├─ census_data
                    ├─ center_lines
                    └─ Index
```

5.8.1 Geodatabase storage in tables and files

Geodatabase storage includes both the schema and rule base for each geographic dataset plus simple, tabular storage of the spatial and attribute data. All three primary datasets in the geodatabase (feature classes, attribute tables, and raster datasets) as well as other geodatabase elements are stored using tables. The spatial representations in geographic datasets are stored as either vector features or as raster. These geometries are stored and managed in attribute columns along with traditional tabular attribute fields.

A feature class is stored as a table. Each row represents one feature. In the polygon feature class table below, the Shape column holds the polygon geometry for each feature. The value Polygon is used to specify that the field contains the coordinates and geometry that defines one polygon in each row.

OBJECTID	SHAPE*	AREA	PERIMETER	NEWC_LU84_UTM_
1941	Polygon	1417540.1	11841.867	2
1942	Polygon	321332.03	3148.0269	3
1943	Polygon	18495728	109063.23	4
1944	Polygon	274196.16	3101.4026	5
1945	Polygon	381471.69	3409.4033	6
1946	Polygon	136670.41	1542.3058	7
1947	Polygon	86315.867	1170.6542	8
1948	Polygon	58589.234	1058.4961	9
1949	Polygon	126296.43	1630.2814	10
1950	Polygon	2177367.8	11357.415	11
1951	Polygon	126567.98	1486.1949	12
1952	Polygon	131079.53	1655.1431	13
1953	Polygon	29051224	116835.71	14
1954	Polygon	851969.69	4640.5933	15
1955	Polygon	189941.86	1732.4786	16
1956	Polygon	195032.53	1994.8439	17
1957	Polygon	50074.400	896.4861	18

A key geodatabase strategy is to leverage the RDBMS to scale GIS datasets to extremely large sizes and numbers of users (for example, to support simple small databases as well as instances with hundreds of millions of features and thousands of simultaneous users). Tables provide the primary storage mechanism for geographic datasets. SQL is very strong at query and set processing of rows in tables, and the geodatabase strategy is designed to leverage these capabilities.

5.8.2 Advanced geographic data types extend feature classes, raster, and attribute tables

Various geodatabase elements are used to extend simple tables, features, and raster to add rich behavior, data integrity, and data management capabilities. The geodatabase schema includes the definitions, integrity rules, and behavior for each of these extended capabilities. These include properties for coordinate systems, coordinate resolution, feature classes, topologies, networks, raster catalogs, relationships, domains, and so forth. This schema information is persisted in a collection of geodatabase Meta tables in the DBMS. These tables define the integrity and behavior of the geographic information.

.

6. Designing geodatabase

6.1 Defining feature class

We should consider the following.

If a spatial type is point:

- for an standalone point (like historical monument) enter a point feature
- for a connected point (like water valve) enter a simple junction feature
- for a connected point with internal structure (like water treatment plant) enter a complex junction feature
- If the spatial type is line:
- for an unconnected line (like fence) enter a simple line feature
- for a line that participates in a system (like road network) enter a simple edge feature
- for a line with connected sections (like water network) enter a complex feature
- If the spatial representation is area:
- for a standalone area (like the parcel) enter a polygon feature
- for a space filling area like vegetation enter a polygon feature with planar topology
- If the spatial type is image (satellite image, scanned map, photograph, etc.) enter a raster type.
- If the spatial feature is a surface:
- for a terrain surface enter a TIN surface representing type

- for a surfaces changing continuously (thermal surface, voice surface, spread of pollution) enter a surface
- If the spatial type is an object and do not have geometric representation (like owner of properties) enter an object type.

Example to match to geodatabase elements:

entity	relation	spatial representation	geodatabase representation
Water utility			
pump	-	point	object
water meter	-	point	point feature
meter box	water meter	point	point feature
valve	-	point	simple junction
main line	--	line	complex edge
treatment plant	-	point	complex junction
Land title			
parcel	-	area	polygon feature
easement	-	line	line feature
parcel record	parcel	text	annotation feature

parcel image	-	image (raster)	raster
owner	parcel	object	object
address of owner	-	location	address
Street network			
street	-	line	line feature
bridge	-	point (line)	point feature
street name	street	text	annotation feature
traffic light	-	point	point feature
bus route	-	line	line feature
bus stop	-	point	point feature
Environment			
monument	-	point	point feature
fence	-	line	line feature
vegetation	-	area	polygon feature
place names	-	text	annotation feature
river valley	-	surface	TIN
satellite image	-	image (raster)	raster

6.2 Creating data type for feature class

When you create feature classes and tables, you select a data type for each field. The available types include a variety of number types, text, date, binary large objects (BLOBs), or globally unique identifiers (GUIDs). Choosing the correct data type allows you to correctly store the data and will facilitate your analysis, data management, and business needs.

If you store your data in an ArcSDE geodatabase or a personal geodatabase, the data types between ArcGIS and your database management system (DBMS) might not match directly. The types are matched to the closest data type available in the DBMS. This process is referred to as data type mapping. In this process, it is possible that the values will be stored in the DBMS as a different type, applying different criteria to the data attribute.

6.3 feature class data type

When creating tables, you will need to select a data type for each field in your table. The available types include a variety of number types, text, date, or binary large object (BLOB). Choosing the correct data type allows you to correctly store the data and will facilitate your analysis, data management, and business needs.

6.3.1 Numeric Data type

Numeric fields can be stored as one of four numeric data types. These include short integers; long integers; single-precision floating point numbers (float); and double-precision floating point numbers (double). Each of these numeric data types varies in the size and method of storing a numeric value.

In numeric data storage, it is important to understand the difference between decimal and binary numbers. The majority of people are accustomed to decimal numbers, a series of digits between 0 and 9 with negative or positive values and the possible placement of a decimal point. On the other hand, computers store numbers as binary numbers. A binary number is simply a series of 0s and 1s in the different numeric data types, these 0s and 1s represent different coded values, including the positive or negative nature of the number, the actual digits involved, and the placement of a decimal point. Understanding this type of number storage will help you make the correct decision in choosing numeric data types.

In choosing the numeric data type, there are two things to consider. First, it is always best to use the smallest byte size data type needed. This will not only minimize the amount of storage required for your geodatabase but will also improve the performance. You should also consider the need for exact numbers versus approximate numbers. For example, if you need to express a fractional number and seven significant digits will suffice, use a float. However, if the number must be more precise, choose a double. If the field values will not include fractional numbers, choose either a short or long integer.

6.3.1 Integers

The most basic numeric data type is the short integer. This type of numeric value is stored as a series of 16 0s or 1s, commonly referred to as 16 bits. Eight bits are referred to as a byte, thus a short integer takes up two bytes of data. One bit states if the number is positive or negative and the remaining 15 translate to a numeric value with five significant digits. The actual numeric value for a short integer is approximately between -32,000 and +32,000. A long integer is a four-byte number. Again, one bit stores the positive or negative nature of the number while the remaining bits translate to a numeric value with 10 significant digits. The actual range for a long integer is approximately between -2 billion and +2 billion. Both short and long integers can store only real numbers. That is to say that you cannot have fractions, or numbers to the right of the decimal place. To store data with decimal values, you will need to use either a float or a double.

- Short integer: Numeric values without fractional values within specific range; coded values.
- Long integer: Numeric values without fractional values within specific range.

6.3.1.2 Float

A float and double are both binary number types that store the positive or negative nature of the number, a series of significant digits and a coded value to define the placement of a decimal point. This is referred to as the exponent value. Floats and doubles are coded in a format similar to scientific notation. For example, if you wanted to represent the number -3,125 in scientific notation, you would say -3.125×10^3 or -3.125E3. The binary code would break this number apart and assign one bit to state that it is a negative number; another series of bits would define the significant digits 3125; another bit would indicate whether the exponent value is positive or negative; and the final series of bits would define the exponent value of 3. A float is a four-bit number and can store up to seven significant digits, producing an approximate range of values between -3.4E-38 to -1.2E38 for negative numbers and from 3.4E-38 to 1.2E38 for positive numbers. A double is an eight-byte number and can store up to 15 significant digits, producing an approximate range of values between -2.2E-308 to -1.8E308 for negative numbers and 2.2E-308 to 1.8E308 for positive numbers.

It is important to note, however, that floats and doubles are approximate numbers. This is due to two factors. First, the number of significant digits is a limiting factor. For example, you could not express the number 1,234,567.8 as a float because this number contains more than the permissible seven digits. In order to store the number as a float, it will be rounded to 1,234,568, a number containing the permissible seven digits. This number could easily be expressed as a double, as it contains less than the permissible 15 significant digits.

There are also some limitations to numbers a binary value can represent. One analogy that can be made would be in expressing fractions versus decimals. The fraction 1/3 represents a particular value. However, if you try to express this number as a decimal, the number will need to be rounded at some point. It could be expressed as 0.3333333, however, this is still an approximation of the actual value. Just as fractions cannot always be expressed as decimals, some numbers cannot be exactly expressed in binary code, and these numbers are replaced by approximate values. One example of such a number is 0.1. This number cannot be expressed as a binary number. However, the number 0.099999 can be expressed in binary. Thus 0.1 would be replaced with an approximate value of 0.099999.

- Float: Numeric values with fractional values within specific range
- Double: Numeric values with fractional values within specific range

6.3.2 Text

A text field represents a series of alphanumeric symbols. This can include street names, attribute properties, or other textual descriptions. An alternative to using repeating textual attributes is to establish a coded value. A textual description would be coded with a numeric value. For example, you might code road types with numeric values assigning a 1 to paved improved roads, a 2 to gravel roads, and so on. This has the advantage of using less storage space in the geodatabase, however, the coded values must be understood by the data user. If you define your coded values in a coded value domain in the geodatabase and associate the domain with the integer field storing your codes, the geodatabase will display the textual description when the table is viewed in ArcMap or ArcCatalog. For more information on coded value domains, see Subtypes and attribute domains.

6.3.3 Date

The date data type can store dates, times, or dates and times. The default format in which the information is presented is mm/dd/yyyy hh:mm:ss and a specification of AM or PM. When you enter date fields in the table through ArcGIS, they are converted to this format.

6.3.4 Blob

A BLOB, or binary large object, is simply some data stored in the geodatabase as a long sequence of binary numbers. Items such as images, multimedia, or bits of code can be stored in this type of field.

6.3.5 Guid

Global ID and GUID data types store registry style strings consisting of 36 characters enclosed in curly brackets. These strings uniquely identify a feature or table row within a geodatabase and across geodatabases. This is how features are tracked in one-way and two-way geodatabase replication. Developers can use them in relationships or in any application requiring globally unique identifiers. In a relationship, if a Global ID field is the origin key, a GUID field must be the destination key. You can add global IDs to a dataset in a geodatabase by right-clicking it in the Catalog tree and clicking Add Global IDs. The geodatabase will then maintain these values automatically. You can create the GUID field as well, but you must maintain its values.

Databases with a native GUID data type, such as personal geodatabases and Microsoft SQL Server, store global ID and GUID values as 16 bytes. Databases without a native GUID data type store them as 38 bytes.

Some notes on global IDs

- GUID fields can be added to geodatabase datasets using the Fields tab on the Properties dialog box of a feature, or the Add Field command in the table window.
- The Add Global ID command is available for stand-alone feature classes, tables, and attributed relationship classes in geodatabases. It cannot be executed on individual datasets in a feature dataset; it can only be run on the entire feature

dataset. It also cannot be run on tables in a database.
- If a Global ID column already exists, the command leaves the old column; it doesn't drop and add a new Global ID column.
- If you add a feature class to a feature dataset in a geodatabase and want to add a Global ID column to it, you need to run the Add Global ID command on the feature dataset. This will add a Global ID column to the new feature class and any feature classes that don't already have a Global ID column. Feature classes already having a Global ID column will remain unchanged.
- Copying and pasting, data extraction, and XML workspace exporting and importing preserve global ID values in the output geodatabase. Other data exporting and importing methods do not preserve these values.

6.3.6 Raster datatype

Unlike a hyperlink that simply links a feature's field to an image; a field of type raster can actually store the raster data within or alongside the geodatabase.

- There are three types of raster data that can be stored in a geodatabase.

6.3.6.1 Dataset

Raster datasets are single images that are stored in the database. These images may be as simple as a single image imported from a file on disk to a large image that has been created by mosaicking or appending multiple images together into a single, large, and seamless image. Thus, inside ArcSDE, a raster dataset is a table with one row, referencing the raster dataset.

OBJECT_ID	Raster	Geometry
1	BLOB	Polygon

A raster dataset can have only one color map and occupies only one row in a business table, since it is essentially one seamless image. It can also be used as an attribute of Features, such as snapshot of a home, associated with a land parcel polygon or a scanned pump diagram, associated with a well point.

A raster dataset should use when

– Continuous analysis and clipping is to be carried out on one large raster– Retaining all areas of overlap is not important
– Retaining metadata of each input is not important
– Fast viewing at any scale.

6.3.6.2 Raster catalog

A raster catalog is a collection of raster datasets. These raster datasets are defined in a table format, where one record represents one raster dataset. A raster catalog is most often used to display adjacent or overlapping raster datasets without having to mosaic them into one large raster dataset.

OBJECT_ID	Raster	Geometry	Cloud Cover %	Acquisition Date
1	BLOB	Polygon1	0	June 15th, 2004

| 2 | BLOB | Polygon2 | 15 | June 15th, 2004 |
| 3 | BLOB | Polygon3 | 10 | June 15th, 2004 |

Each raster dataset in a raster catalog maintains its own properties. For example, one raster dataset might have a different colormap than another raster, or one might have a different number of bands than another. Raster Catalogs can accommodate a different colormap for each raster dataset, but the projection needs to be the same for each dataset. If geoprocessing tools are used to load raster datasets into raster catalogs, each raster dataset will be automatically reprojected to the projection of the raster catalog.

A raster dataset inside a raster catalog behaves in the same way as a stand-alone raster dataset. Therefore, you can mosaic raster data into a raster dataset that resides in a raster catalog.

A raster catalog should be used when:

– Overlapping areas of individual inputs are important
– Metadata of individual inputs is important
– Query on attributes/metadata (i.e. % cloud cover)
– Simply want to keep/store individual images

6.3.6.3 An attribute of type raster

With ArcGIS 10x, feature class or stand-alone tables can contain a column of type RASTER. A RASTER type column can contain any supported image, picture, or raster dataset, such as digital photos of a feature or a scanned floor plan. Only one RASTER column can be defined for a particular feature class or table.

When a raster is stored in a RASTER column, it is converted to an ArcSDE Raster format and stored in the geodatabase.

7. FIELD WORK

7.1 Ground control point collection

Garmin GPS is a device used for navigation. This device can record points, lines and give route information. This device works in all weather conditions and gives accurate results.

Garmin GPS is mainly for the heavy duty mapping and because of this reason it requires comprehensive training for the most accurate data collection. This device provides capability for military, civil and commercial users all over the world.

7.2 Use of base map

Field paper is a tool which help you in creating a multipage atlas of different places anywhere in the world. Field paper helps in collecting data quickly with less efforts in the field as significant amount of data has been already uploaded to Open Street map (OSM). OSM is a collection of maps all over the world and can be edited by freely by anyone. You can take its print out and that can be use in the field to record the information about the area and you can also use it as a guide paper in unknown places.

The field paper are not recommended where the existing data records are too poor for the further process. In this case person should personally record the data accurately of the additional places on the map.

7.2 Defining data

In geographical data there are three types of Data

POINTS: Point is a symbol used to represent a particular type of location on the earth. By the latitude and longitude coordinates this location is described. A point can represent a power pole, telephone box and a house. On any GPS device, points can be collected by using point functions.

LINES: line represent linear features and described by a series of points in the path. Line can represent routes, rivers, roads, cables and to outer line the area. On any GPS device, lines can be collected by using tracking feature.

POLYGONE: polygon is a bounded self-contained area. Polygon represent the outline of the particular area like school boundary, a street area, house, building footprint. Polygons are not as easier to collect as points and lines in GPS device.

7.3 Methodology used
7.3.1 GENERAL

- Allot the job of survey field manager to a person from the team.
- In the team every person who collects data should have a GPS device.
- Transportation in the rural areas increases the work efficiency, if possible every data collector should have motorized transport

- Field map of completed base map are used by taking print outs, and these field pages should distribute to every data collector
- Note the technical steps to follow for the reference, technical steps can be (Example: how to switch on device, how to record points or lines with device, etc.)
- Note the methodologies for reference
- Make the daily record of data collectors and the device they are using.
- Data collectors can show their collection of data at the end of the day and go through it and if any error founds should improve/correct it, it maintains the quality of work
- It's important to make more copies of data collection paper because it is unavoidably become dirty and ruined in the field work.

7.3.2 TIME MANAGEMENT AND COVERAGE

- Divide the assessment area in the sections in respect to the surveyors and alot the each part of area to a different surveyor. Division should be done on the atlas paper
- For each day make a work plan to achieve the specific target to access the coverage area.
- Each day before starting the work, volunteers should gather and should assigned by the new target and devices.
- After completing the day work, gather volunteer's devices, examine the data collected

and present them the results of the day. Recognize the errors and faults in the data collection

7.3.3 DATA ORGANIZATION

- Make a list of points of interest (POIs) define the data types you want like points, lines, polygons.
- Select a standard location from where the points can be taken which are relative to each type of POI's
- Provide additional information for each feature collection.
    1. Road name, type and material
    2. Construction materials of bridge (steel, wood)
    3. Places of meeting (meeting point, under a tree, in schoolyard)
    4. Disaster durable example: buildings or block strengthened to secure from disaster like earthquake or flooding.

Data collection table

POI	Data Type	Name Format Example	Notes Regarding Collection	Attribute 1	Attribute 2	Attribute 3	Attribute 4

8. Building geodatabase

8.1 Creating Geodatabase and Feature dataset

The Geodatabase has three different kinds of data sets to manage geographic information. Creating and developing these above mentioned data sets are the primary need to design and build a new Geodatabase. Users have to start first with these datasets designs later on the user can also add the advance features in the Geodatabase like one can add topology and network design. The storage of the Geodatabase has both the schema and the set of rules for every datasets and a table like storage for spatial attribute and data.

Steps:

Creating a new file geodatabase using ArcCatalog

- Open ArcCatalog. Right-click the file folder in the ArcCatalog tree where you want to create the new file geodatabase.
- Point to New.

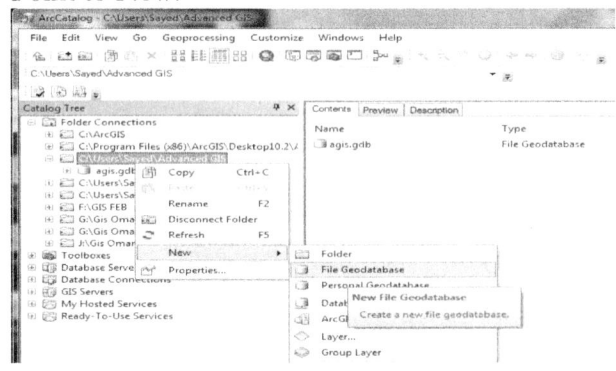

- Click File Geodatabase. ArcCatalog creates a new file geodatabase in the location you selected.
- Rename the new file geodatabase to AGIS by right-clicking on the new file geodatabase and choosing Rename.

A feature dataset is a collection of related feature classes that share a common coordinate system. Feature datasets are used to spatially or thematically integrate related feature classes. Their primary purpose is for organizing related feature classes into a common dataset for building a topology, a network dataset, a terrain dataset, or a geometric network.

Use feature datasets to organize spatially related feature classes into a common dataset:
- To Add a Topology
- To Add a Network Dataset
- To Add a Geometric Network
- To Add a Terrain Dataset

There are additional situations in which users apply feature datasets in their geodatabases:

To organize thematically related feature classes

Sometimes, users will organize a collection of feature classes for a common theme into a single feature dataset. For example, users might have a feature dataset for Water that contains Hydro Points, Hydro Lines, and Hydro Polygons.

To organize data access based on database privileges

Sometimes, users organize data access privileges using feature datasets. All feature classes contained within a feature dataset have the same access privileges. For example, users might need to use more than one feature dataset to segment a series of related feature classes to account for differing access privileges between users. Each group has editing access to one of the feature datasets and its feature classes, but no edit access for the others.

To organize feature classes for data sharing

In some data sharing situations, collaborating organizations might agree on a data sharing schema for sharing datasets with other users. In these situations, people might use feature datasets as folders to organize collections of simple feature classes for sharing with others.

Specifying the coordinate system up front

Another design factor in organizing feature classes into common feature datasets is the requirement to use a spatial reference. Thus, it's useful to define your coordinate system requirements for each feature class prior to organizing feature classes into common feature datasets.

When creating a new feature dataset, you must define its spatial reference. This includes its coordinate system—either geographic or a specific projection—as well as coordinate units and tolerances for xy, z-, and m-values. All feature classes in the same feature dataset must share a common coordinate system, and xy coordinates of their features should fall within a common spatial extent.

Steps to create feature dataset
1. In the Catalog tree, right-click the geodatabase in which you want to create a new feature dataset.
2. Click New > Feature Dataset.

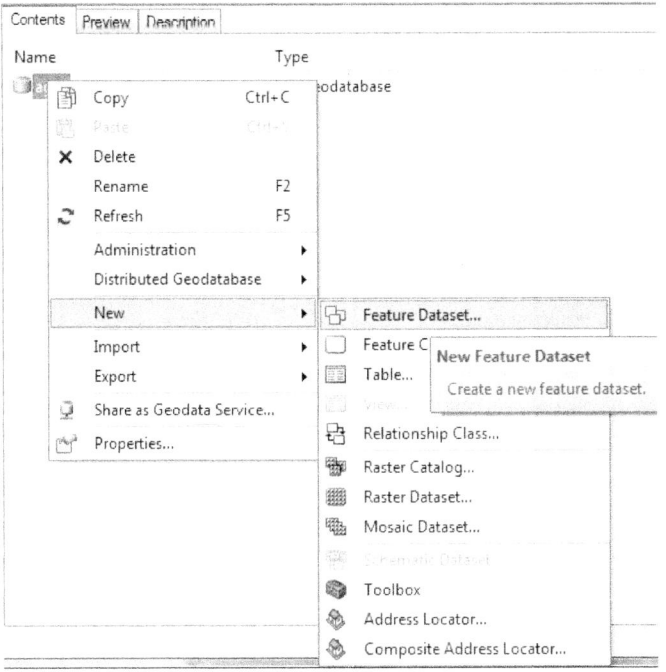

MAPPING IN GIS

Contents	Preview	Description		
Name			Type	

[Context menu showing:]
- Copy   Ctrl+C
- Paste
- Delete
- Rename   F2
- Refresh   F5
- Administration ▶
- Distributed Geodatabase ▶
- New ▶
- Import ▶
- Export ▶
- Share as Geodata Service...
- Properties...

[Submenu:]
- Feature Dataset...
- Feature Class
- Table...
- View...
- Relationship Class...
- Raster Catalog...
- Raster Dataset...
- Mosaic Dataset...
- Schematic Dataset...
- Toolbox
- Address Locator...
- Composite Address Locator...

[Tooltip: New Feature Dataset — Create a new feature dataset.]

3. Type a name for the feature dataset.

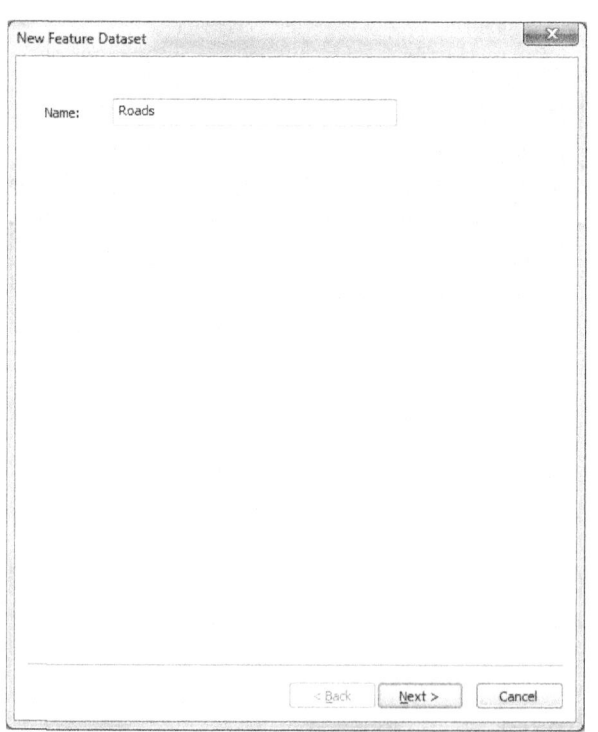

> **New Feature Dataset**
>
> Name: Roads
>
> [< Back] [Next >] [Cancel]

4. Navigate to the spatial reference you want to use. Alternatively, click Import and navigate to the feature class or feature dataset that uses the spatial reference you want to use as a template.

MAPPING IN GIS

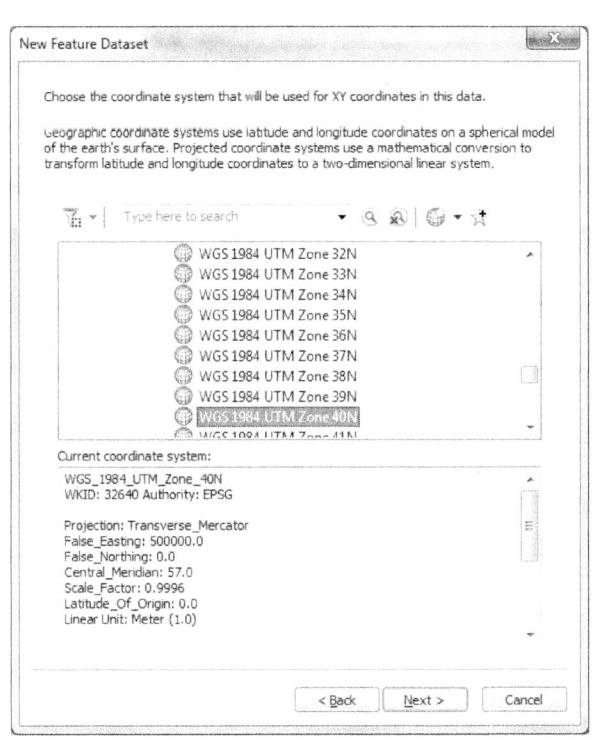

5. Use Modify if you want to change any parameters in the coordinate system you've chosen. Edit the coordinate system's parameters and click OK.

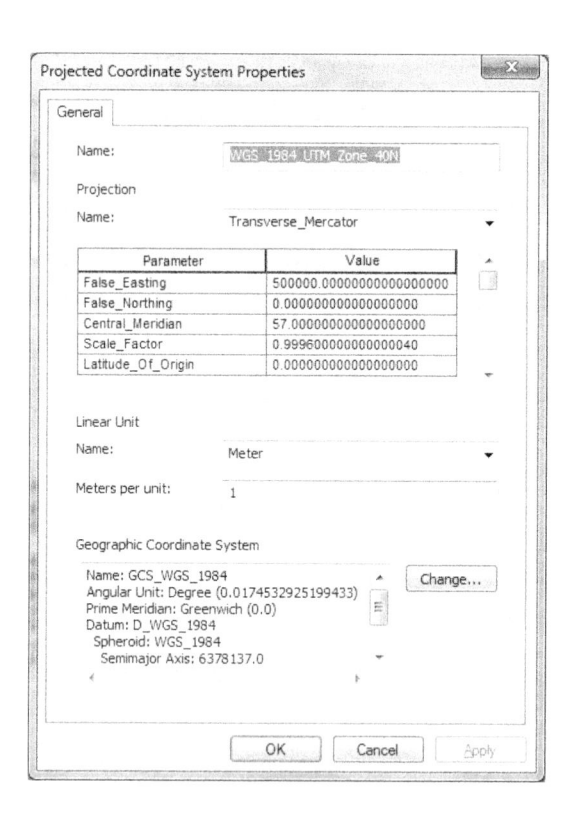

Projected Coordinate System Properties

General

Name: WGS_1984_UTM_Zone_40N

Projection

Name: Transverse_Mercator

Parameter	Value
False_Easting	500000.00000000000000000
False_Northing	0.00000000000000000
Central_Meridian	57.00000000000000000
Scale_Factor	0.99960000000000040
Latitude_Of_Origin	0.00000000000000000

Linear Unit

Name: Meter

Meters per unit: 1

Geographic Coordinate System

Name: GCS_WGS_1984
Angular Unit: Degree (0.0174532925199433)
Prime Meridian: Greenwich (0.0)
Datum: D_WGS_1984
 Spheroid: WGS_1984
  Semimajor Axis: 6378137.0

6. If your data requires a vertical coordinate system for z-units, you may import one from another feature class or feature dataset; otherwise, select None. Click Modify if you want to change any parameters in the coordinate system you've chosen. Edit the coordinate system's parameters and click OK.

7. Enter values for the xy-tolerance, z-tolerance, and m-tolerance, or accept the default value, which is the equivalent of 1 mm in real-world units.

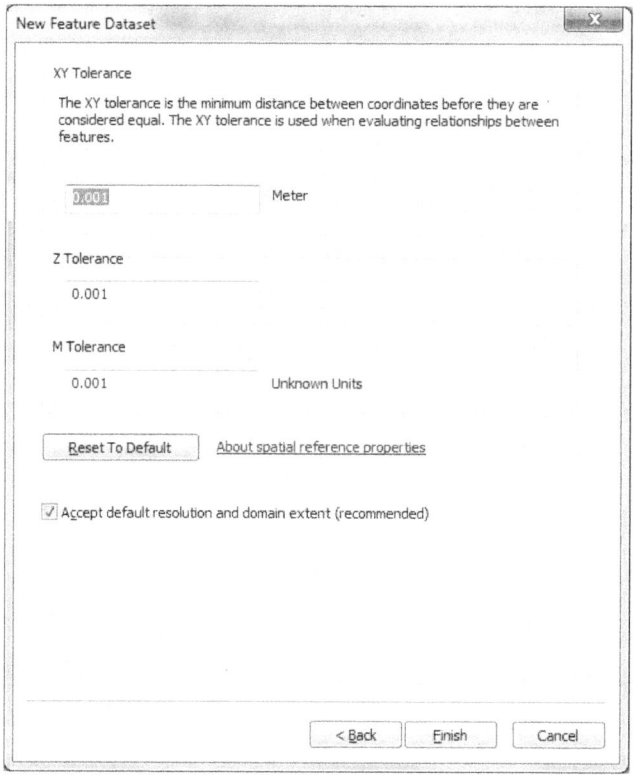

8. Your feature data set is ready now
   - C:\Users\Sayed\Advanced GIS
     - agis.gdb
       - Roads

8.2 Creating Feature class

You can perform Geoprocessing tasks on the feature classes contained within a geodatabase feature dataset. Geodatabase feature classes store geographic features represented as points, lines, polygons, annotation, dimensions, and multipatches and their attributes. They store simple features, so they can be organized inside or outside a feature dataset, but always inside a geodatabase, personal or ArcSDE. Simple feature classes that are outside a feature dataset are called standalone feature classes. Feature classes that store topological features must be contained within a feature dataset to ensure a common coordinate system.

Feature classes hold the homogenous collection of the same features, where each feature has same spatial representation like points, lines and polygons with a similar set of attribute column. For example a point representing some specific location, a line feature class representing roads lines. Points, lines, polygons and annotations are the most commonly used feature classes used in Geodatabases. Along with these feature classes Vector features for representing geographic object with vector geometry are frequently used for representing discrete boundaries like walls, streets and rivers.

In simple words we can say that a feature is simply an object which holds the graphical representation and which we typically a collection of point, line and polygon.

Following are the features classes used to hold the graphical representation of an object:

- **Points**: This class is used to represent features that are very small (such as a GPS observation).
- **Lines**: This class is used to represent shape and location of geographic objects Eg. Street lines and streams, or we can use this class to represent those graphical objects which have length but no area.
- **Polygons**: This class is used to represent shape and location of geographic objects Eg. States, countries and land use zone etc.
- **Annotation**: This is used to show some descriptive properties of geographic objects. This class is responsible for text rendering for graphical objects.

8.2.1 Creating a feature class in a feature dataset

1. In the Catalog tree, right-click the feature dataset in which you want to create a new feature class.
2. Point to New > Feature Class.

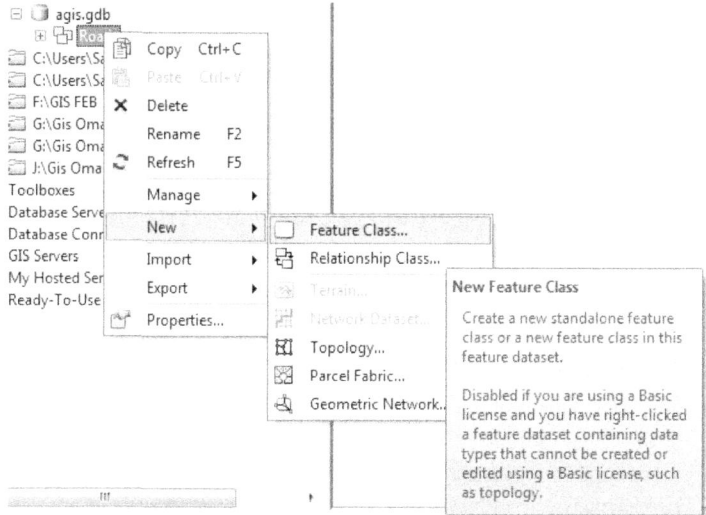

3. Type a name for the feature class. To create an alias for this feature class, type the alias.
4. Choose from the drop-down list the type of features that will be stored in this feature class.
5.

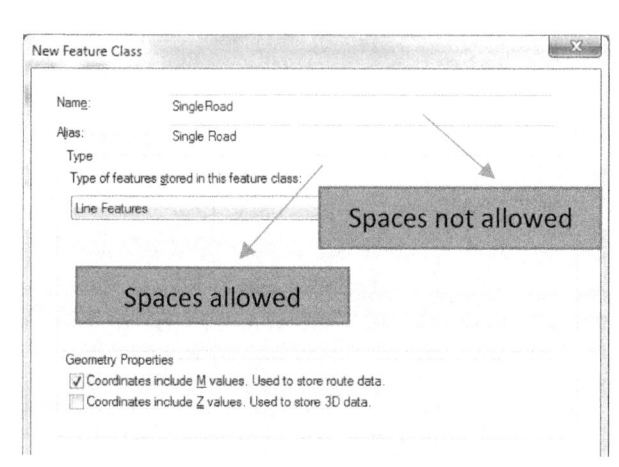

6. If your data will require m- or z-values, check the appropriate check boxes.
7. Click Next.
8. If any feature class in the feature dataset will have measures, enter a value for M tolerance or accept the default.

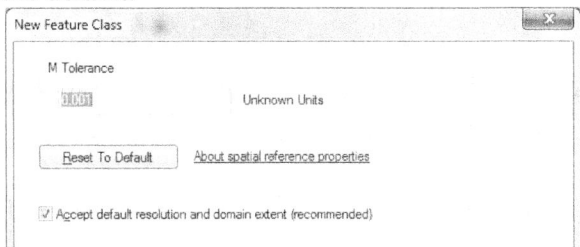

9. By default, the Accept default resolution and domain extent check box is checked. If you want to manually adjust the resolution and domain extent values of your new dataset, uncheck this box. If you are creating data in a pre-9.2 geodatabase or chose Unknown for the horizontal coordinate system, you should uncheck this box and confirm that the default values are appropriate. If you have unchecked the Accept default resolution and domain extent check box, there is an additional panel in the wizard that allows you to change the M resolution as well as the minimum and maximum m-values.
10. If your geodatabase is not a file or ArcSDE Enterprise geodatabase, skip to step 11. If you want to create the table using a custom storage keyword, click Use configuration keyword and specify the keyword you want to use.
    (NoteNote:This is available in ArcGIS for Desktop Advanced and Standard only.)
11. Click Next.

12. To add a field to the feature class, click the next blank row in the Field Name column, then type a name.
13. Click the Data Type column next to the new field's name and click its data type.
14. To create an alias for this field, click the field next to Alias and type the alias for this field.
15. To prevent nulls from being stored in this field, click the field next to Allow nulls, click the drop-down arrow, and then click No.
16. To associate a default value with this field, click the field next to Default value and type the value.
17. To associate a domain with this field, click the field next to Domain, click the drop-down arrow to see a list of the domains that apply to this field type, then click the domain.
18. To set other properties specific to the type of field, either click the property in the drop-down list or type the property.

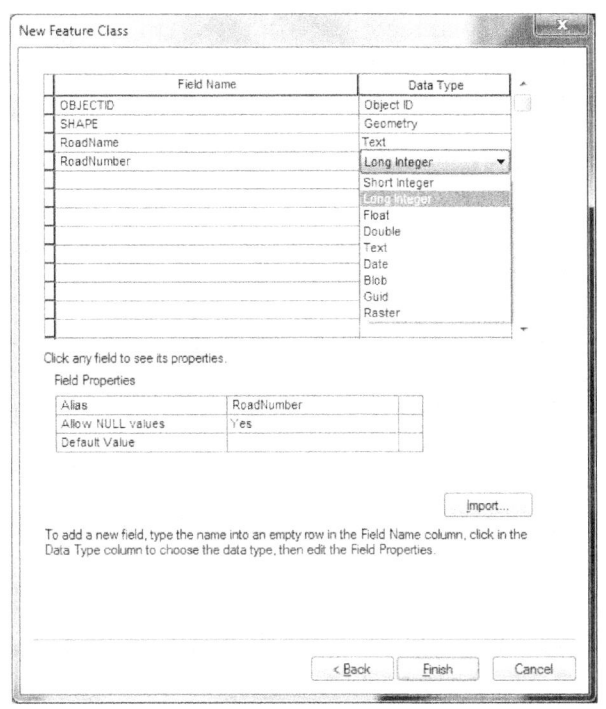

19. Repeat steps 11 through 17 until all the feature class fields have been defined.
20. If you want to import field definitions from another feature class or table, click Import.
21. Click Finish.

8.2.2 Creating Standalone feature class

1. In the Catalog tree, right-click the geodatabase in which you want to create a new feature class.
2. Point to New > Feature Class.
3. Type a name for the feature class. To create an alias for this feature class, type the alias.
4. Choose from the drop-down list the type of features that will be stored in this feature class.
5. If your data will require m- or z-values, check the appropriate check boxes.
6. Click Next.

7. Navigate to the spatial reference you want to use or click Import and navigate to the feature class or feature dataset that uses the spatial reference you want to use as a template.
8. Click Modify if you want to change any parameters in the coordinate system you've chosen. Edit the coordinate system's parameters and click OK.
9. If your data requires a vertical coordinate system, you may import one from another feature class or feature dataset; otherwise, select None. Click Modify if you want to change any parameters in the coordinate system you've chosen. Edit the coordinate system's parameters and click OK.
10. Enter an x,y-tolerance or accept the default value. The default x,y-tolerance is 1 mm on the Earth's surface at the point of projection.
11. If any feature class in the feature dataset will have z-values, enter the z-tolerance or accept the default.
12. If any feature class in the feature dataset will have measures, enter the m-tolerance or accept the default.
13. If you've changed the x,y-; z-; and/or m-tolerances and want to revert to the default values, click the Reset all tolerances button.
14. By default, the Accept default resolution and domain extent check box is checked. If you want to manually adjust the resolution and domain extent values of your new dataset, uncheck this box. If you are creating data in a pre-9.2 geodatabase or chose Unknown for the horizontal coordinate system, you should uncheck this box and confirm that the default values are appropriate.
15. If you have unchecked the Accept default resolution and domain extent check box, there is

an additional panel in the wizard that allows you to change the M resolution as well as the minimum and maximum m-values.
16. If your geodatabase is not a file or ArcSDE geodatabase, skip to step 18. If you want to create the table using a custom storage keyword, click Use configuration keyword and specify the keyword you want to use. NOTE: This is available in ArcGIS for Desktop Advanced and Standard only.
17. Click Next.
18. To add a field to the feature class, click the next blank row in the Field Name column, then type a name.
19. Click the Data Type column next to the new field's name and click its data type.
20. To create an alias for this field, click the field next to Alias and type the alias for this field.
21. To prevent nulls from being stored in this field, click the field next to Allow nulls, click the drop-down arrow, then click No.
22. To associate a default value with this field, click the field next to Default value and type the value.
23. To associate a domain with this field, click the field next to Domain, click the drop-down arrow to see a list of the domains that apply to this field type, then click the domain.
24. To set other properties specific to the type of field, either click the property in the drop-down list or type the property.
25. Repeat steps 18 through 24 until all the feature class fields have been defined.
26. Click Import if you want to import field definitions from another feature class or table.
27. Click Finish.

8.2.3 Feature Class Representation

To represent feature class in a geodatabase, normally we use Symbology to show them. When you want to specify a certain rule for symbology, you can define rules using Feature Representation Tab as follows.

Feature class representations symbolize layers in a framework that is stored and accessible from within the source geodatabase. Representations can be used as the basis for layer display, dictating how the features of the source feature class should be symbolized.

There may still be reasons why you would want to save layer files. If your feature class has more than one representation associated with it, a layer file can reference a specific representation, eliminating the need to convey that information to anyone you share the data with. There are also a number of layer properties that are stored within a layer file that you may want to preserve, such as scale ranges, definition queries, and labeling rules.

Symbolizing a layer with a representation

The representation rules that dictate how groups of features will be symbolized in a representation can be viewed and modified—along with other representation settings—from the Symbology tab on the Layer Properties dialog box.

A layer symbolized with a feature class representation

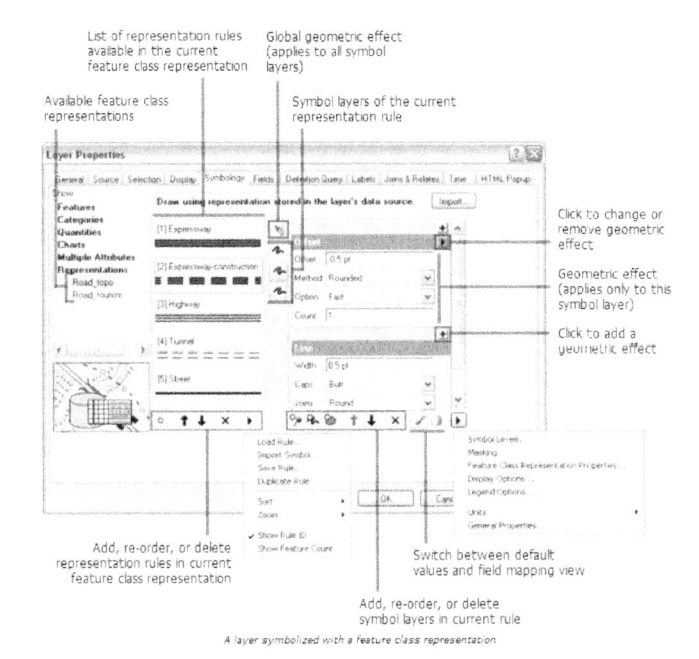

How to symbolize a layer with a representation

1. Click Properties on the shortcut menu of the layer containing the representation to open the Layer Properties dialog box.
2. Click the Symbology tab.
3. If the feature class referenced has any associated representations, the Representations heading will be visible on the left pane of the dialog box.
4. Click this heading to see the list of representations associated with the feature class this layer references. If there is no Representations heading, there are no representations associated with this feature class.
5. Choose a representation from the list and modify the representation rules, if necessary.
6. Click OK to symbolize the layer with the selected representation.

Setting representation visibility

Visibility is a property of a feature class representation. That is, all representation rules in a feature class representation will respect the same visibility setting; it cannot be set independently for individual representation rules. However, it is a property that can be overridden for individual features. Typically, you keep the default setting of the visibility property on. Then, you can override this setting in an edit session, making individual feature representations invisible as necessary.

To gain more control over the visibility property, you can map it to an explicit field in your feature class to dictate which feature representations will be visible. The field you reference can contain a short or long integer data type, with values of 1 representing a visible state and values of 0 representing invisible.

To modify the shape or other properties of invisible feature representations, you need to be able to see them somehow in your map. To achieve this, you can display all invisible feature representations with a distinctive color. This option is turned off by default. When you turn it on, invisible feature representations are shown in gray by default. Similarly, features that do not have a valid (or have a NULL value) RuleID are displayed by default in red. Adjust either of these settings by clicking the Layer Options button Layer Options button and choosing Display Options on the Symbology tab on the Layer Properties dialog box. The layer must be symbolized with a feature class representation for this button to be visible. These settings are properties of the layer inside the map document; they are not saved with the feature class representation.

How to change the visibility of a feature class representation

1. Click Properties on the shortcut menu of the layer containing the representation to open the Layer Properties dialog box.
2. Click the Symbology tab.
3. If the feature class referenced has any associated representations, the Representations heading will be visible on the left pane of the dialog box.
4. Click this heading to see the list of representations associated with the feature class this layer references. If there is no Representations heading, there are no representations associated with this feature class.
5. Choose a representation from the list, click the Layer Options button Layer Options button, then choose General Properties.
6. Check or uncheck the Visibility check box to draw or hide all feature representations in the feature class representation by default. This visibility setting can be overridden on a feature-by-feature basis during an edit session.

How to set the visibility based on a field in the feature class

1. Click the Display Field Overrides button Representation property mapped to an explicit field on the Layer Properties dialog box to switch to field mapping view. Choose a field from the drop-down list that holds Boolean values indicating visibility. This field can be either short- or long-integer, where values of 1 indicate visible and values of 0 indicate invisible.
2. Click OK to save the settings.

How to display invisible feature representations

1. Click Properties on the shortcut menu of the layer containing the representation to open the Layer Properties dialog box.
2. Click the Symbology tab.
3. If the feature class referenced has any associated representations, the Representations heading will be visible on the left pane of the dialog box.
4. Click this heading to see the list of representations associated with the feature class this layer references. If there is no Representations heading, there are no representations associated with this feature class.
5. Choose a representation from the list, click the Layer Options button Layer Options button, then choose Display Options.
6. Check Draw invisible representations and choose a distinctive color to display them.

How to disp lay feature representations that have NULL or invalid rules

1. Click Properties on the shortcut menu of the layer containing the representation to open the Layer Properties dialog box.
2. Click the Symbology tab.
3. If the feature class referenced has any associated representations, the Representations heading will be visible on the left pane of the dialog box.
4. Click this heading to see the list of representations associated with the feature class this layer references. If there is no Representations heading, there are no representations associated with this feature class.
5. Choose a representation from the list, click the Layer Options button Layer Options button, then choose Display Options.
6. Check Draw representations that have an invalid or null RuleID and choose a distinctive colour to display them.

Using representation feature-level masking

One of the advantages of symbolizing your data with representations is that you can control masking on individual features rather than at the layer level. By setting up a relationship class between a new polygon layer and a feature class representation, you can control the masking of individual features, groups of features, and even portions of features.

How to enable masking in a feature class representation

1. Create a new polygon feature class to hold your masks.
2. Create a many-to-many relationship class between this new feature class and the feature class that contains the feature class representation that you want to mask.
3. In ArcMap, click Properties on the shortcut menu of the layer containing the representation to open the Layer Properties dialog box.
4. Click the Symbology tab.
5. If the feature class referenced has any associated representations, the Representations heading will be visible on the left pane of the dialog box.
6. Click this heading to see the list of representations associated with the feature class this layer references. If there is no Representations heading, there are no representations associated with this feature class.
7. Choose a representation from the list, click the Layer Options button Layer Options button, then choose Masking.
8. Check the check box next to the new feature class you just created to activate the masking relationship.
9. The mask polygon feature class does not need to be added to the map as a layer. You may want to add it to see the masks as they are created. You create individual masks in an edit session.

8.2.4 Creating a new feature class by saving the contents of a map layer in ArcMap

If you are working with a dataset in ArcMap, you can export it to create a feature class or a shapefile.
1. Right-click the dataset in the Table Of Contents that you would like to export. This brings up the context-sensitive menu.
2. Click Data > Export Data.

This brings up the Export Data dialog box.

If you are working with a dataset in ArcMap, you can export it to create a feature class or a shapefile.
1. From the drop-down list, choose whether you would like to export all features or just those in the view extent.
2. Choose one of three radio button options for which coordinate system the exported dataset will inherit. These include the following:
   - The same coordinate system as the data source referenced by the layer you are exporting
   - The coordinate system of the data frame (ArcMap) or scene (ArcScene) to which the layer you are exporting belongs
   - The coordinate system of the feature dataset into which you choose to export data
1. Specify the output data you would like to create.

Do one of the following:

Type the name of the output directly into the field. It will be saved in the current output location. Move the cursor over the Browse button to get a tip showing you the current output location. (If the current location is a file geodatabase, it will have a .gdb extension; if it's a personal geodatabase, it will have an .mdb extension; if it's an ArcSDE Personal or Workgroup geodatabase on a database server, it will have a .gds extension; if it's a connection to a spatial database, it will have an .sde extension).

Or:

Click Browse and use the browser to specify the location and name of the output data.

If you save the output to a folder (e.g., a directory on disk), it will be saved as a shapefile. You can use spaces in the shapefile name. If you don't specify a .shp extension, ArcMap will automatically add it for you.

If you save the output into a geodatabase (a file, personal, or ArcSDE geodatabase), it will be saved as a geodatabase feature class. You cannot use spaces in the name of a feature class.

8.2.4 Copying Schema

A schema defines the physical structure of the geodatabase along with the rules, relationships, and properties of each dataset in the geodatabase. Defining and implementing a practical schema for a geodatabase is an important task that often requires prototyping and testing of a proposed design. Testing will help you to develop a robust, working system implementation.

Once you have a workable geodatabase schema, you'll find many reasons for creating a copy of the entire schema or parts of it. For example:

- Users often share their schemas with others.

- Data model templates exist for many GIS application domains. For example, ESRI publishes a series of ArcGIS data models for the user community. See

- Users want to make multiple copies of their geodatabase schemas for use in various departments.

- Users want to compare their schemas with their collaborators.

Therefore, it's a good idea to become familiar with tools that can be used to copy and share geodatabase schemas.

There are a number of alternative mechanisms, which are described here, that can be used to copy a geodatabase schema.

Steps:

1. Start ArcMap.
2. Click the Add Data button to add a map layer using a dataset from the geodatabase whose schema you want to export.
3. Open the Distributed Geodatabase toolbar: click View > Toolbars > Distributed Geodatabase.

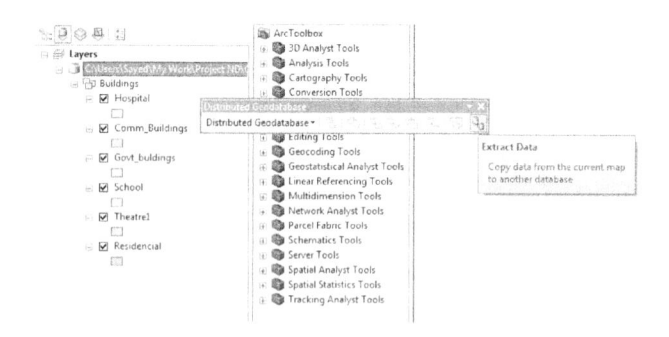

4. Click Extract Data on the Distributed Geodatabase toolbar to start Extract Data Wizard.
5. Click the Schema Only button in response to the question, what do you want to extract?
6. Navigate to the geodatabase into which you want to copy the schema or type its path. If the geodatabase doesn't already exist, it will be created for you.

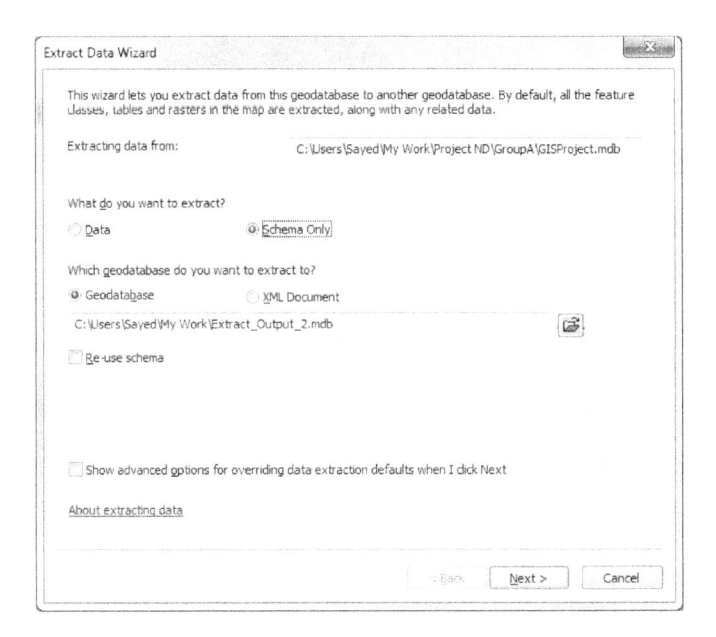

7. Check the Show advanced options for overriding data extraction defaults when I click Next choice at the bottom of the Extract Data Wizard dialog box.

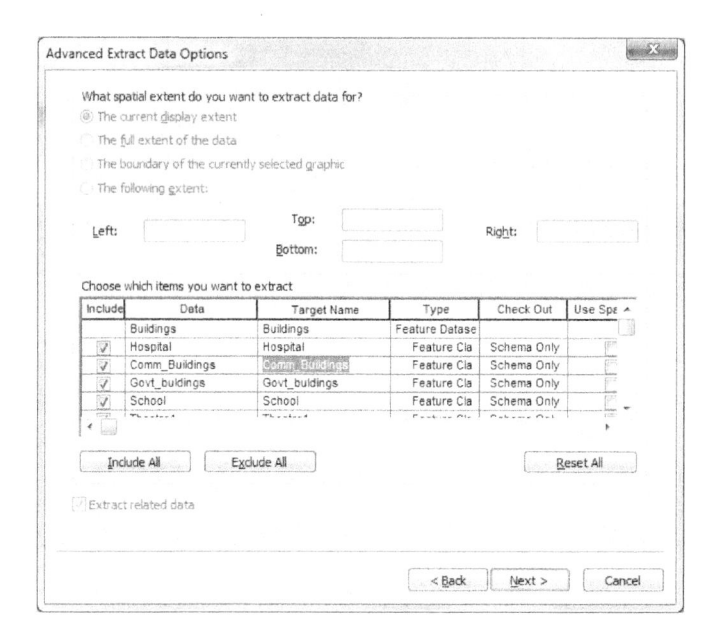

8. Click Next to preview the contents of the schema information to be copied.

   This panel lists all the data items whose schema information will be copied.

9. Uncheck the Include check boxes for the feature classes, tables, or relationship classes whose schemas you don't want to export.

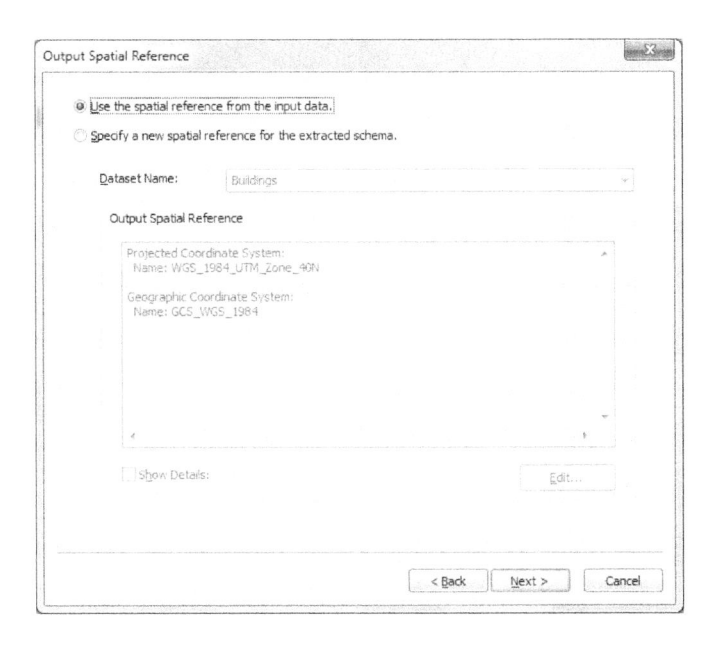

If you leave a box checked for a feature class in a network, topology, or a terrain, the schemas for all the feature classes participating in the network, topology, or terrain are copied. Click Next.

10. On this panel, you have the option to specify a new spatial reference for the output schema.

If you want to set a different spatial reference for the output schema, check the specify a new spatial reference for the extracted schema option. The spatial reference you choose will be used for all the datasets you extract. Click Next.

If you want the output schema to keep the same spatial reference as the source data, simply click Next.

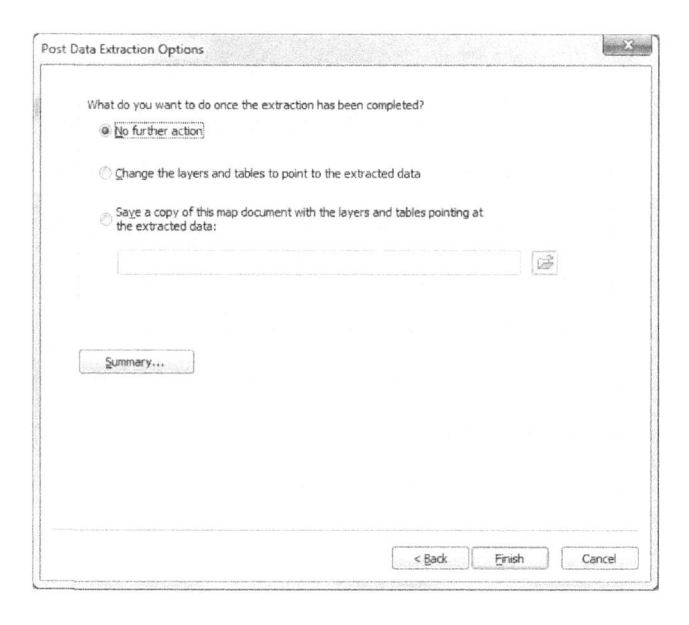

11. In this final panel, review a summary of the extraction contents and other optional settings. When you are ready, click Finish to export the schema.

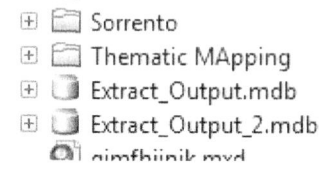

⊞ 🗀 Sorrento
⊞ 🗀 Thematic MApping
⊞ 🗀 Extract_Output.mdb
⊞ 🗀 Extract_Output_2.mdb
   aimfhiinik mxd

8.2.5 Modifying field data types

Modifying field data type has 3 issues
1. Modifying data type of empty feature class
   - It is possible to change data type of empty feature class

- To do so, select feature class from catalog tree and go to properties

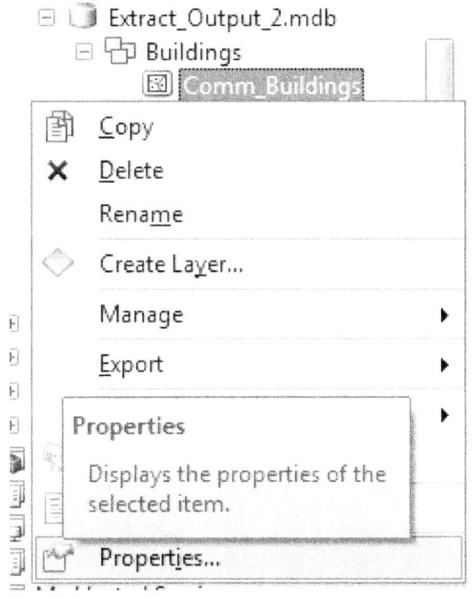

```
⊟  Extract_Output_2.mdb
   ⊟  Buildings
        Comm_Buildings
```

- Copy
- Delete
- Rename
- Create Layer...
- Manage ▶
- Export ▶
- Properties

  Displays the properties of the selected item.

- Properties...

7 Select/change from list of data type available

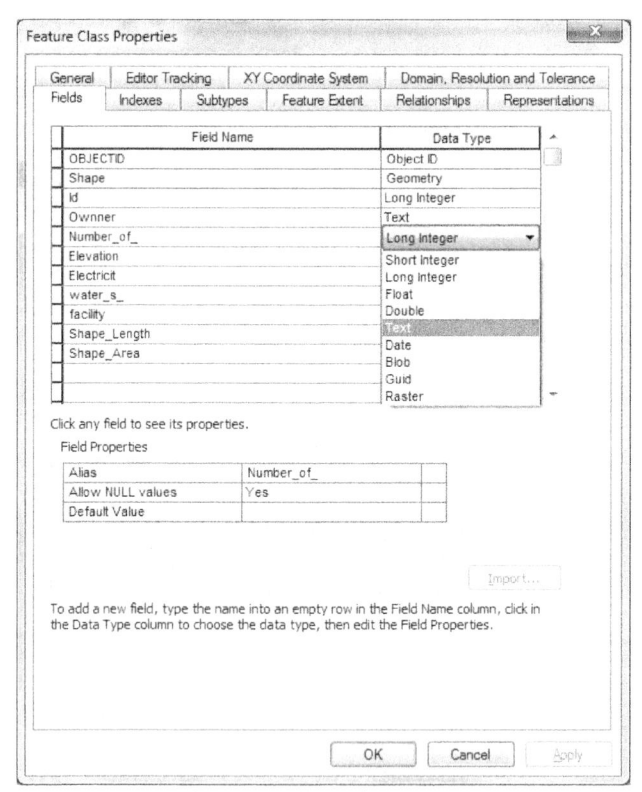

(Here we are changing from long integer to Text)
8   Press ok to finish. Data type will be change
   1. Modifying data type of filled feature class
9   It is not possible to change data type of feature class having attributes.
10   You may get the following error message

11 This is because, one cannot change the data type from table having attributes.

9. Migrating your existing data into the Geodatabase

9.1 Importing data into the geodatabase

- In the Catalog tree, select the geodatabase you want to place your GIS data into, right-click and select Import from the context menu, then choose the appropriate data import tool.

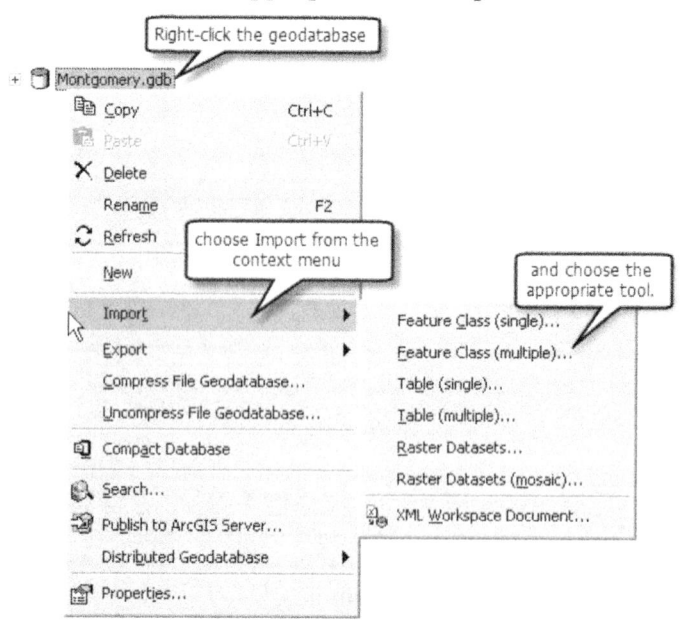

- Select feature class single
- You will get the following dialog box

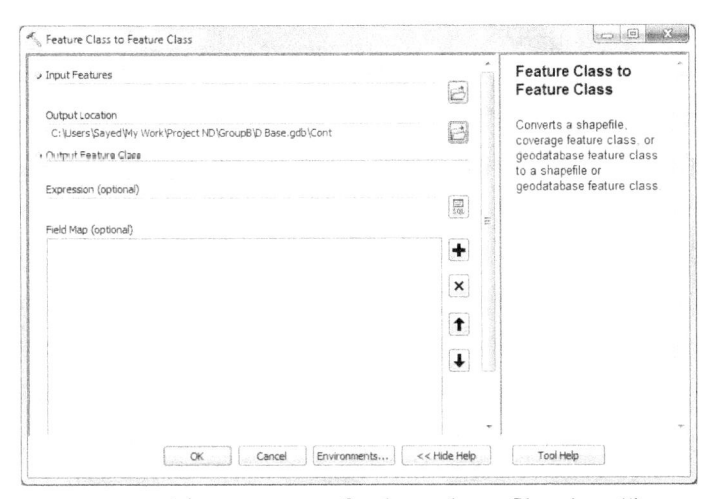

- provide name of the shapefile in "input features", give output name and press ok
- your feature class will be imported

9.2 Exporting data into the geodatabase

- In the Catalog tree, browse to and select the GIS dataset that you want to put into the geodatabase, right-click and select export from the context menu, then choose the appropriate data export tool.

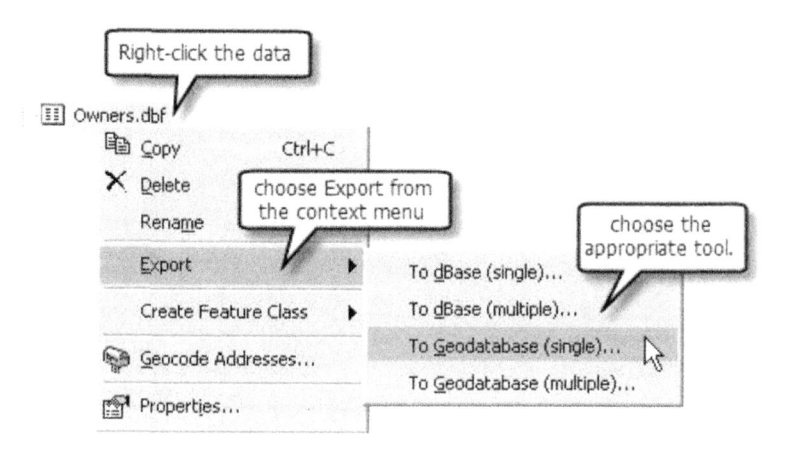

[Screenshot showing right-click context menu on Owners.dbf with annotations: "Right-click the data", "choose Export from the context menu", "choose the appropriate tool." The menu shows Copy, Delete, Rename, Export (with submenu: To dBase (single), To dBase (multiple), To Geodatabase (single), To Geodatabase (multiple)), Create Feature Class, Geocode Addresses, Properties.]

- Select "to shapefile""

- The following dialog box will appear

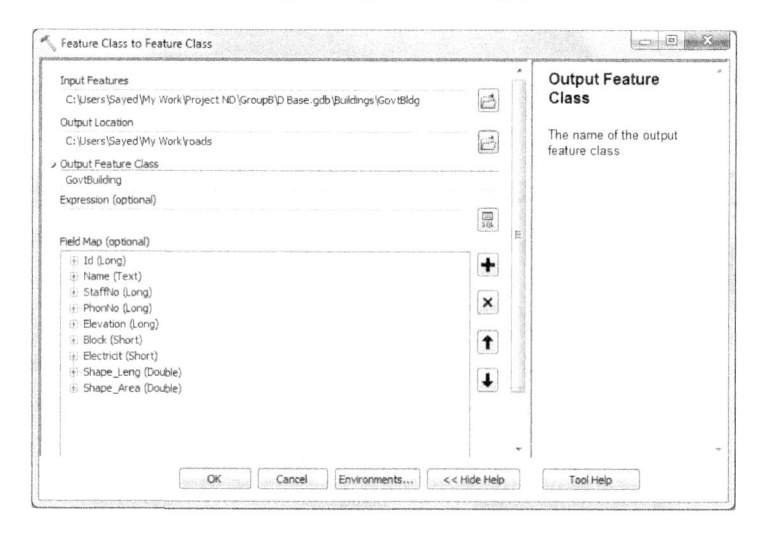

[Screenshot of "Feature Class to Feature Class" dialog box with Input Features, Output Location, Output Feature Class (GovtBuilding), Expression (optional), and Field Map (optional) listing Id (Long), Name (Text), StaffNo (Long), PhonNo (Long), Elevation (Long), Block (Short), Electricit (Short), Shape_Leng (Double), Shape_Area (Double).]

- Provide of the select ""output location" and "output feature class", then press ok

- Feature class will be exported

9.3 Migrating Shapefiles into a Geodatabase
9.3.1 Feature class to feature class

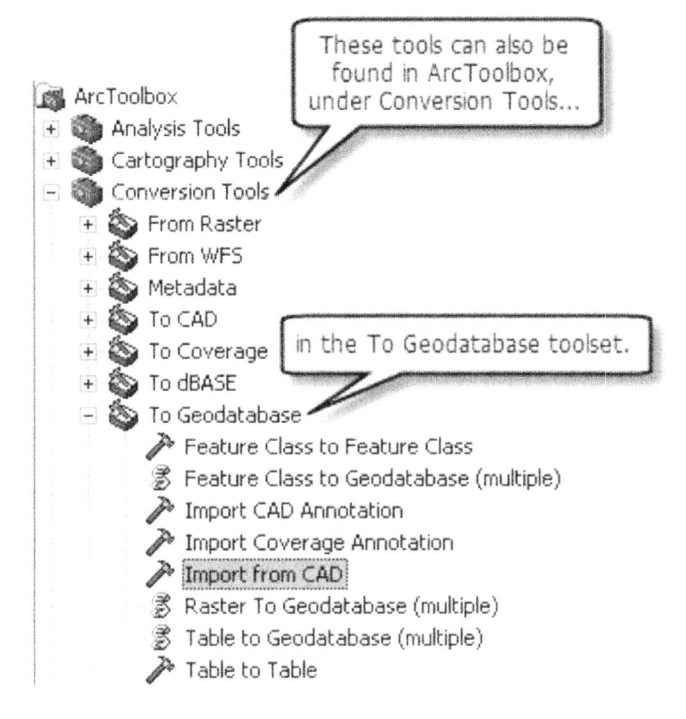

These tools can also be found in ArcToolbox, under Conversion Tools... in the To Geodatabase toolset.

You will need to specify the following:

- Input Features – you can browse to a shapefile or drag and drop one into the input box.

- Output location – this can be the geodatabase or a feature dataset within the geodatabase. Again you can browse to a location or drag and drop one into the input box

- Output Feature Class – the name of the output feature class that will be created.

There are also 3 optional input parameters:

- Expression – enables you to define a SQL expression to select a subset of the rows in the input table to migrate.

- Field Map – provides options to add, rename, or delete fields when the input shapefile is converted to the output feature class.

- Configuration Keyword – this is used to specify storage parameters in ArcSDE geodatabases and File geodatabases.

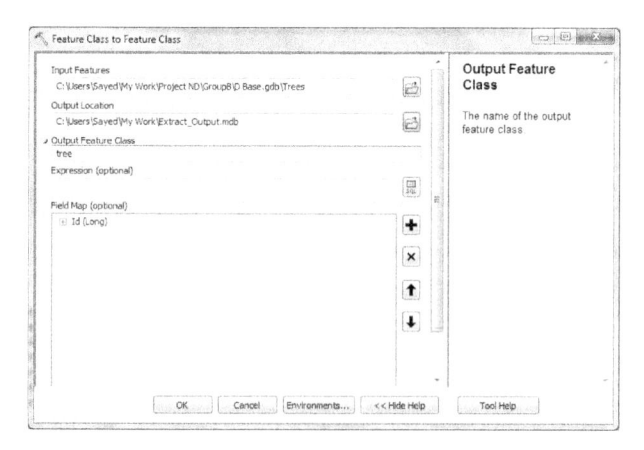

For the Field Map parameter, we recommended that you drop the FID, shape_length, and shape_area attribute fields, because these will be replaced by new fields when the shapefile becomes a feature class in the geodatabase.

9.3.2 Feature class to geodatabase

The Feature Class to Geodatabase tool works on multiple shapefiles. Idealy you would use this tool over the Feature Class to Feature Class tool if you had many shape files to migrate to a Geodatabase. To use this tool you specify one or more shapefiles to convert and the output geodatabase location. By default, the shapefiles will have the same names as the original shapefiles when they are migrated into the geodatabase.

10. Joins and Relates

10.1 Rational for Using Related Tables

The relational database model offers many advantages for managing data. These include the maintenance of independent data structures, the fact that such relationships model reality, and transaction management. The flexibility of the relational structure is superior to so-called flat file approaches which present normalization problems and lead to redundancy in your data.

Among the most common uses for related tables in ArcGIS is the "lookup table". This is a table containing additional attributes for features stored in an associated feature attribute table. An example would be symbolizing surface geology types with accepted symbols. There would be many polygons with the same geologic attribute (type) and one additional table that crosswalks the geologic type to a particular map symbol. This would be a "many-to-one" type of relate. Another reason for using a lookup table may be the need to associate feature data with data maintained by other groups.

10.2 Cardinalities in Relations

Cardinality specifies how many instances of an entity relate to one instance of another entity. Cardinality affects the types of associations used in ArcMap.

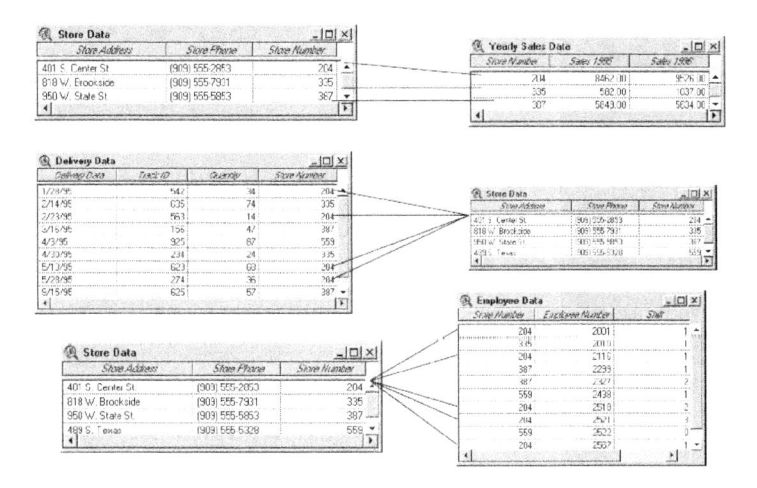

A relationship between two objects is maintained through attribute values for key fields.

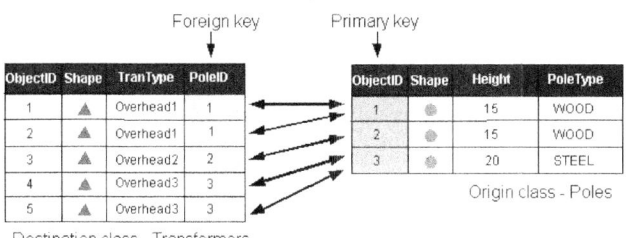

10.3 Types of File associations in ArcGIS

ArcMap provides two methods of associating data stored in tables. The first of these is the join. The join results in the appending the fields of one table to those of another through an attribute or field common to both tables. This is commonly used to attach more attributes to the attribute table of a geographic layer. One can join two tables when the data in the tables has a one-to-one or a many-to-one relationship.

The second type of file association is the relate. The relate is an operation that establishes a temporary connection between records in two tables using an item common to both. Relate two tables when the data in the tables has a one-to-many or many-to-many relationship. Joins and relates are reconnected whenever you open the map, so if the underlying data in your tables changes, it will be reflected in the join or relate. When you're through using a join or relate, you can remove it. It exists in the application, not in the database.

10.4 Special Features of Joins in ArcGIS

A spatial join is a type of table join operation in which fields from one layer's attribute table are appended to another layer's attribute table based on the relative locations of the features in the two layers. Such joins use locations of objects to find:
- The closest feature to another feature.
- What's inside a feature?
- What intersects a feature?
- How many points fall inside each polygon?

How, then, does this differ from feature-based selection common in applications like ArcMap and ArcView 3.x? "Select by location" provides a returned set of features and symbolizes them in a default selection symbol. A spatial join, on the other hand, provides a more permanent association between the two layers because it creates a new layer containing both sets of attributes.

10.5 Other Types of File associations Supported by ArcGIS Other ArcGIS

If you are using a geodatabase for your spatial data, you can access an additional method of associating tables, without establishing a "relate" in ArcMap. This method relies on the definition of a "relationship class" in the geodatabase. Relationship classes are declared and defined and would automatically be available in ArcMap when you add a layer

that participates in a relationship class to the map.
Geodatabase relationship classes are usually created to establish an enduring business process relationship between a feature class and another table or feature class. ArcMap joins and relates are useful in data building, data exploration, or analysis.

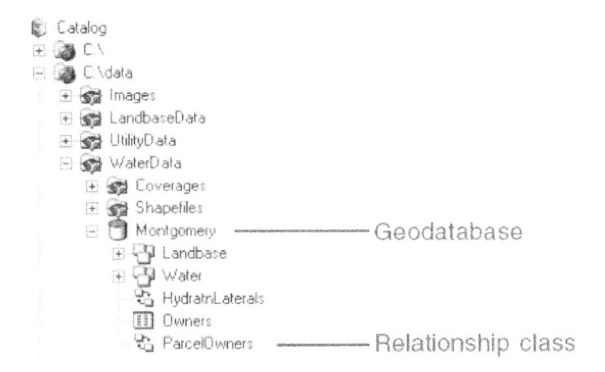

Relationship classes appear in the ArcCatalog tree either at the geodatabase level or inside a feature dataset.

10.5 Join and relating tables

Most database design guidelines promote organizing your database into multiple tables—each focused on a specific topic—instead of one large table containing all the necessary fields. Having multiple tables prevents duplicating information in the database, because you store the information only once in one table. When you need information that isn't in the current table, you can link the two tables together.

For example, you might obtain data from other departments in your organization, purchase commercially available data, or download data from the Internet. If this information is stored in a table, such as a dBASE, INFO, or geodatabase table, you can associate it with your geographic features and display the data on your map.

ArcGIS allows you to associate records in one table with records in another table through a common field, known as a key. You can make these associations in several ways, including by joining or relating tables temporarily in your map or by creating relationship classes in your geodatabase that maintain more permanent associations. For example, you could associate a table of parcel ownership information with the parcels layer, since they share a parcel ID field.

When you join two tables, you append the attributes from one onto the other based on a field common to both. Relating tables defines a relationship between two tables—also based on a common field—but doesn't append the attributes of one to the other; instead, you can access the related data when necessary.

10.6 Joining the attributes from a table

Typically, you'll join a table of data to a layer based on the value of a field that can be found in both tables. The name of the field does not have to be the same, but the data type has to be the same; you join numbers to numbers, strings to strings, and so on. You can perform a join with either the Join Data dialog box, accessed by right-clicking a layer in ArcMap, or the Add Join tool.

Suppose you have obtained data that describes the percentage change in population by county and you want to generate some population growth maps based on this information. As long as the population data is stored in a table in your database and shares a common field with your layer, you can join it to your geographic features and use any of the additional fields to symbolize, label, query, or analyze the layer's features.

10.6.1 One-to-one and many-to-one relationships

When you join tables in ArcMap, you establish a one-to-one or many-to-one relationship between the layer's attribute table and the table containing the information you want to join. The example below illustrates a one-to-one relationship between each county and that county's population change data. In other words, there's one population change for each county.

Here's an example of a many-to-one relationship. Suppose you have a layer where each polygon is classified according to its land-use type. The layer's attribute table only stores a land-use code; a separate table stores the full description of each land-use type. Joining these two tables establishes a many-to-one relationship because many records in the layer's attribute table join to the same record in the table of land-use descriptions. You might then use the more descriptive text when generating the legend for your map.

MAPPING IN GIS

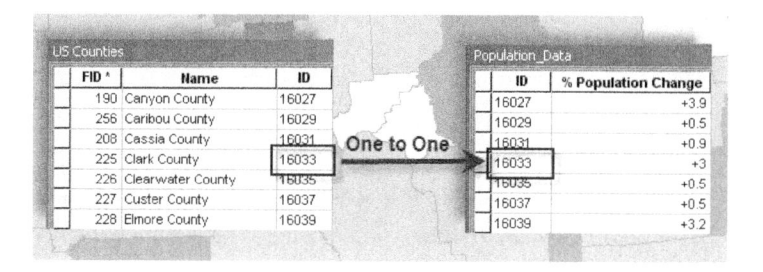

US Counties				Population_Data	
FID	Name	ID		ID	% Population Change
190	Canyon County	16027		16027	+3.9
256	Caribou County	16029		16029	+0.5
208	Cassia County	16031	One to One	16031	+0.9
225	Clark County	16033		16033	+3
226	Clearwater County	16035		16035	+0.5
227	Custer County	16037		16037	+0.5
228	Elmore County	16039		16039	+3.2

10.6.2 One-to-many and many-to-many relationships

When using data where a one-to-many or many-to-many relationship exists, you should use a relate or relationship class to establish the relationship between the datasets. However, it is possible to create a join under these circumstances. When you create a join in such a case, there are differences between how tools and other layer-specific settings work depending on the data source. If you are using geodatabase data to create the join, all matching records are returned. If you are using nondatabase data, like shapefiles or dBASE tables, to create the join, only the first matching record is returned.

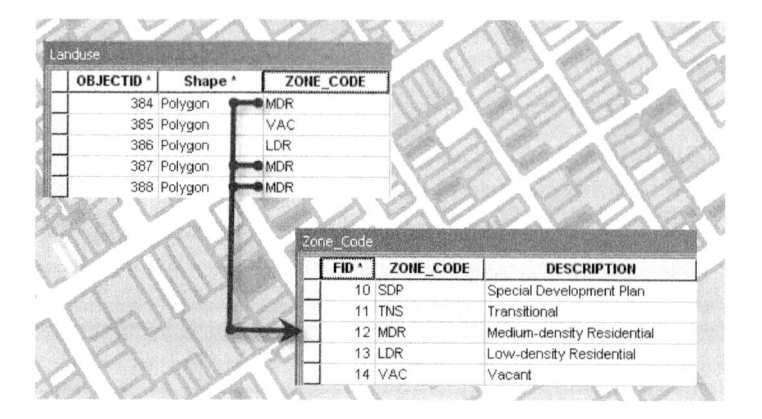

Landuse		
OBJECTID	Shape	ZONE_CODE
384	Polygon	MDR
385	Polygon	VAC
386	Polygon	LDR
387	Polygon	MDR
388	Polygon	MDR

Zone_Code		
FID	ZONE_CODE	DESCRIPTION
10	SDP	Special Development Plan
11	TNS	Transitional
12	MDR	Medium-density Residential
13	LDR	Low-density Residential
14	VAC	Vacant

This means that if you have created a 1:M or M:M join

with geodatabase data and you generate a report, you see multiple records in the report, one for each corresponding match. The multiple matches are also seen when using a join field while symbolizing a joined layer, labeling, identifying features, generating a graph, and using either the Find or Hyperlink tool. If you are using the joined layer as input to a Geoprocessing tool or in an export operation, the multiple matching records are used.

10.7 Practical – Joining Table
Steps:

1. First open Arcmap and add your data. Open the attribute table of High_way feature class and see the attributes of this feature.

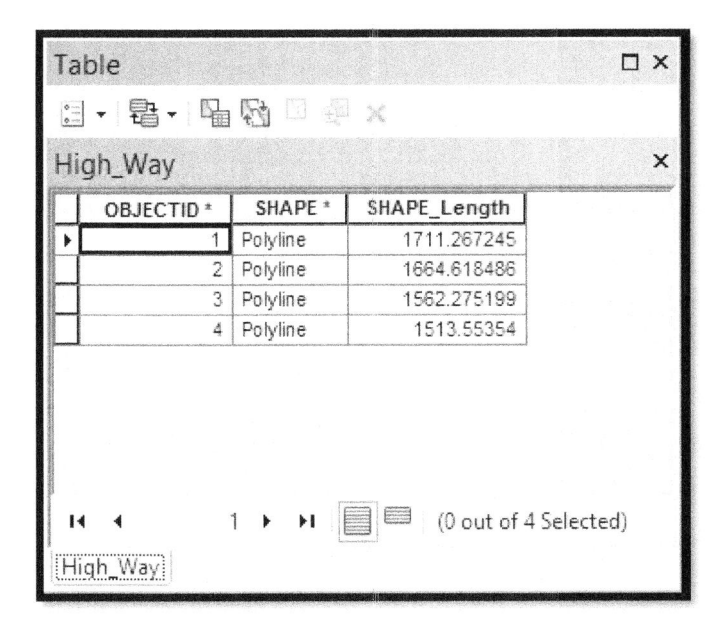

OBJECTID	SHAPE	SHAPE_Length
1	Polyline	1711.267245
2	Polyline	1664.618486
3	Polyline	1562.275199
4	Polyline	1513.55354

(0 out of 4 Selected)

We only have three fields on this table. We have the

other data on excel file which describes the other specifications for this particular feature.

2. Now we need to join that table to the one here so that we could see it as one table having the full description of a desired feature.
3. Right click on High_way feature class and go to join and relates and choose join from the list.

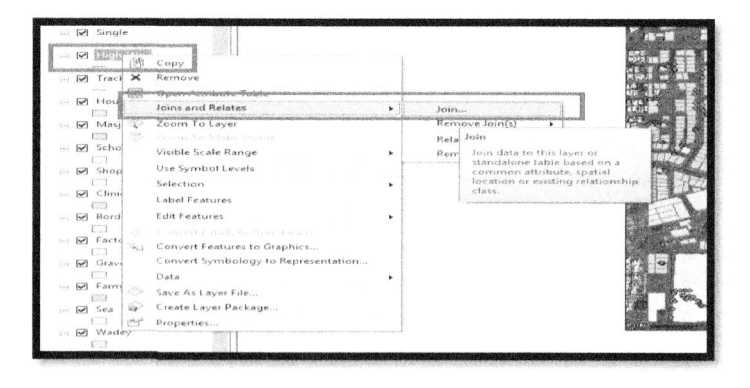

4. On the join data window, set the file as the figure below. Browse to your excel file where you save it.

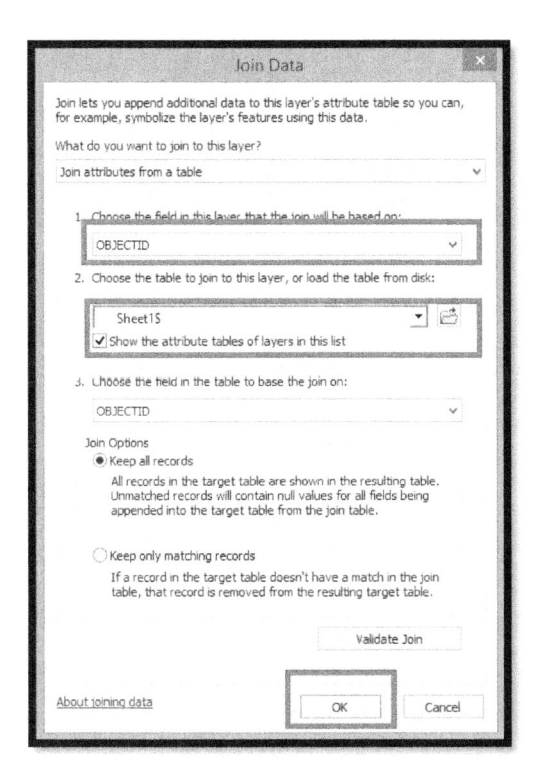

5. Open the attribute table of High_way feature class and see the new data been added.

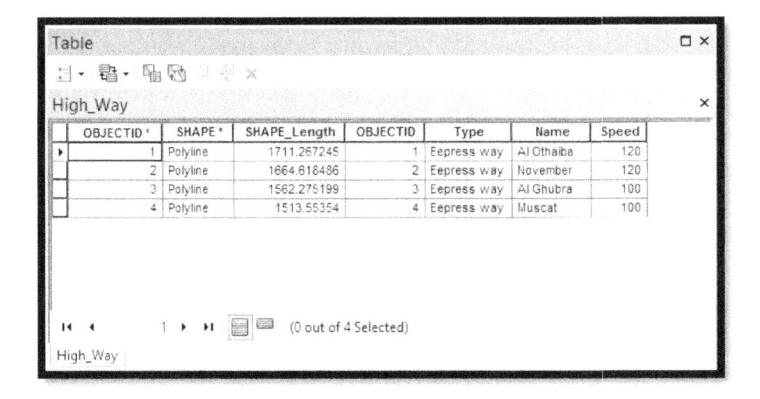

11. Annotations in geodatabase

11.1 What is annotation?

Annotation in the geodatabase is stored in annotation feature classes. As with other feature classes, all features in an annotation feature class have a geographic location and attributes and can either be inside a feature dataset or a standalone feature class. Each text annotation feature has symbology including font, size, color, and any other text symbol property. Annotation is typically text, but it can also include graphic shapes—for example, boxes or arrows—that require other types of symbology.

11.2 Types of annotation

There are three types of geodatabase annotation:

- Standard annotation
- Feature-linked annotation
- Dimension annotation

11.2.1 Standard annotation

Standard annotation feature classes exist independently of other feature classes. No permanent relationship exists between the annotation and the features they describe.
Standard annotation is useful if you want to create annotation that reflects the state of a database at different times or conditions or to label areas on your map where features don't exist in your database. For example, you could create standard annotation to show the land use for parcels over a period of years or to label the oceans of the world even though there are no ocean

features in your database.

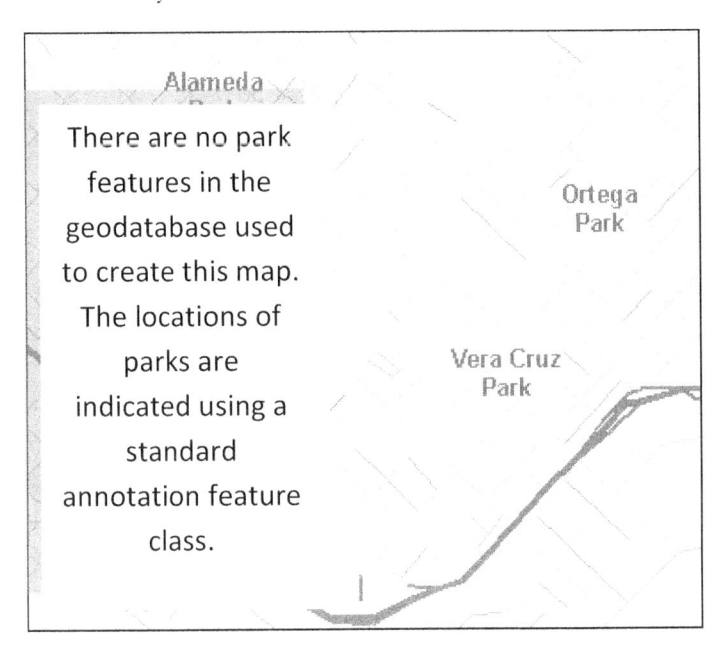

> Alameda
>
> There are no park features in the geodatabase used to create this map. The locations of parks are indicated using a standard annotation feature class.
>
> Ortega Park
>
> Vera Cruz Park

11.2.2 Feature-linked annotation

Feature-linked annotation is associated with features in another feature class. When you move the geographic features, the annotation moves with them. If you delete a feature, its annotation is automatically removed, and if you change the feature attribute used to create the annotation, the annotation text changes as well.

With feature-linked annotation, the annotation updates when the feature it is linked to changes. In this example, when the Crestline, Bel Air, and Rialto Street features are edited, the street

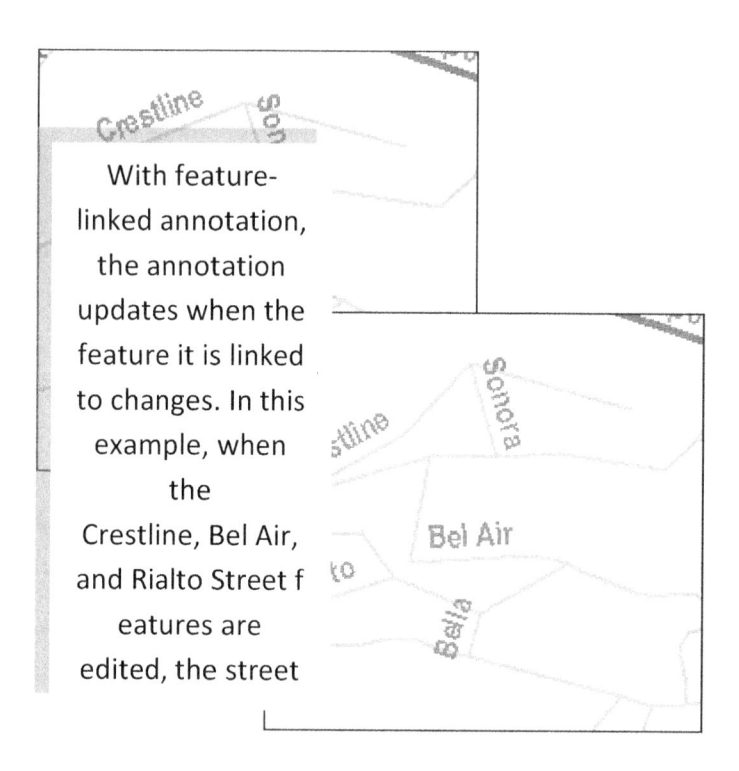

11.2.3 Dimension annotation

Dimensions are a special kind of annotation used to display specific lengths or distances on a map. They are stored as features in dimension feature classes.

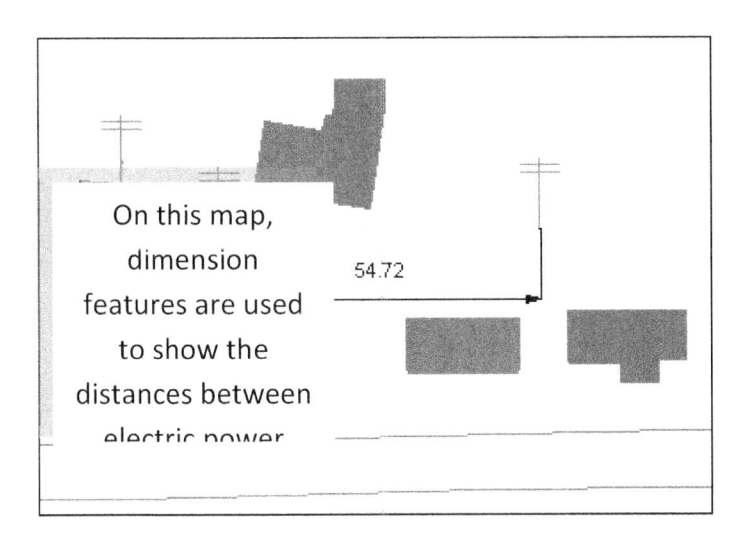

On this map, dimension features are used to show the distances between electric power

11.3 Creating annotations
11.3.1 Creating annotation feature class

1.1 In the Catalog tree, right-click the feature dataset in which you want to create the new annotation feature class.

1.2 Point to New > Feature Class.

1.3 Type the Name.

1.4 Optionally, type an Alias.

1.5 Click the Type drop-down arrow and click Annotation Features.

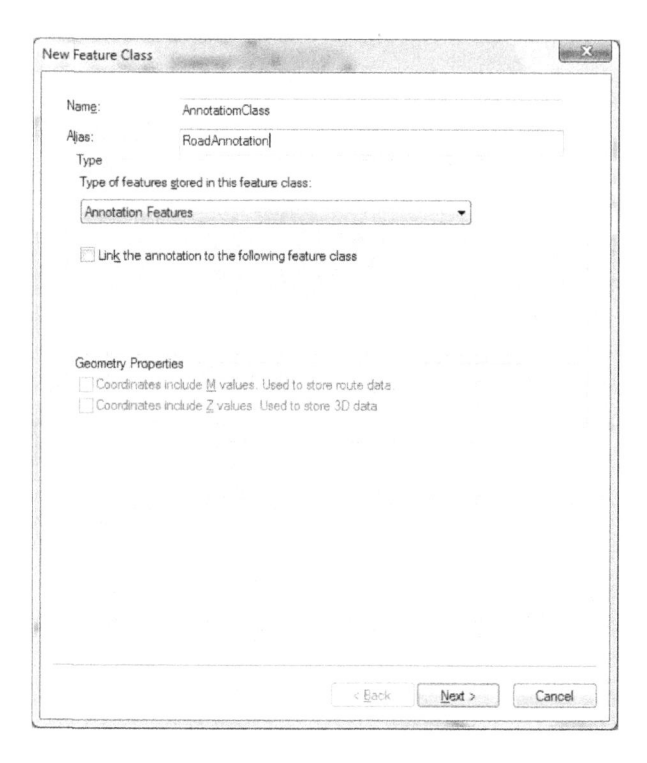

[New Feature Class dialog box screenshot showing Name: AnnotatiomClass, Alias: RoadAnnotation, Type: Annotation Features, with Geometry Properties and navigation buttons]

1.6 Click Next.

1.7 Click the Reference scale drop-down arrow and select a scale, or type in a scale value.

1.8 The scale should be equal to the scale at which the annotation will normally display.

1.9 Map units are automatically set for you, because the annotation feature class is inside a feature dataset. The units match the units of the feature dataset's coordinate system. If the feature dataset coordinate system is unknown, the units default to meters.

1.10   Optionally, check Require symbol to be selected from the symbol table.

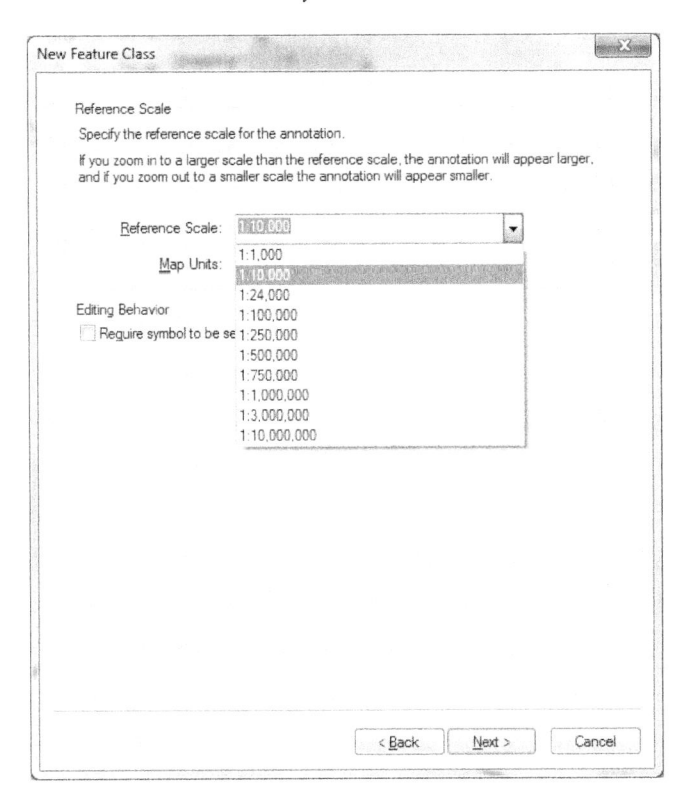

1.11   Click Next.

1.12   For Text Symbol, set the default text symbol properties for the first annotation class.

1.13   Specify the visible Scale Range for annotation in this class.

1.14   If you want to add an additional annotation class, click New and type the Name of the annotation class. Repeat steps 10 and 11 to set its properties.

MAPPING IN GIS

1.15   Repeat step 12 until you have specified all the annotation classes and their properties.

1.16   Click Next.

1.17   If you are creating the new annotation feature class in a file or ArcSDE geodatabase, and you want to use a custom storage keyword, click Use configuration keyword, then choose from the drop-down list the keyword you want to use. If you don't want to use a custom storage keyword, leave the Default.

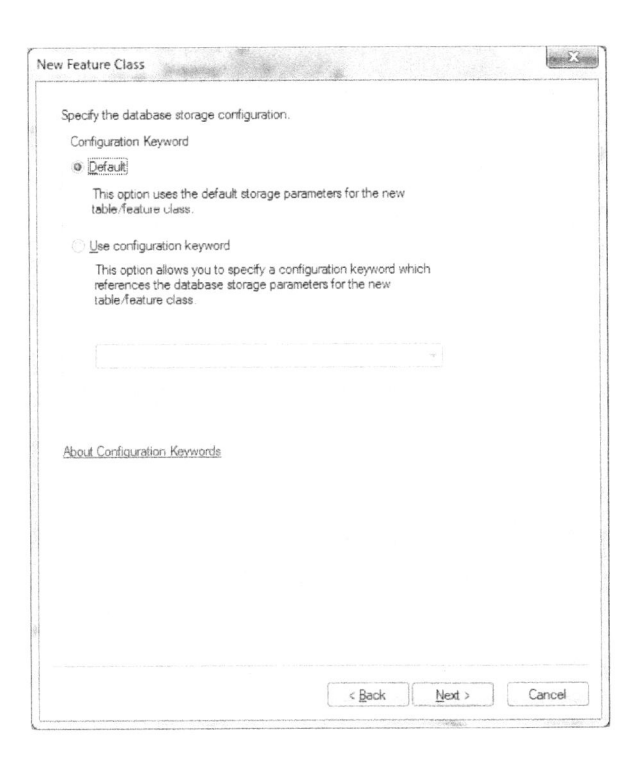

1.18 Click Next.

1.19 You don't have to change any of the field properties. The feature class resides in a feature dataset, so the spatial reference will automatically be that of the feature dataset.

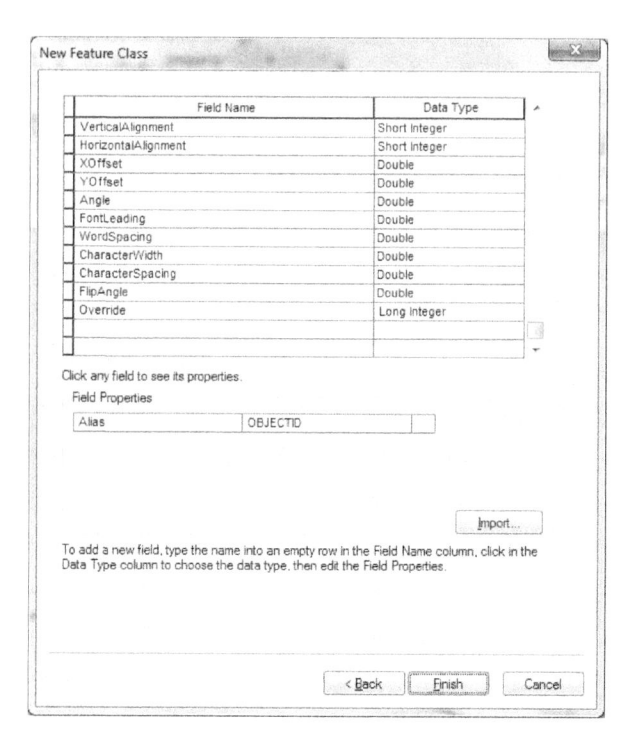

1.20   Click Finish.

11.3.2 Creating Annotation features

The Create Features window and the Editor toolbar provide the tools you need to create new annotation features. The Create Features window allows you to choose the construction method for your new annotation—horizontal, curved, leader line, and so on. Once you choose the tool to use, the Annotation Construction window appears, so you can enter the text of the new annotation, control how the text is placed, and override the default annotation properties as defined by the feature template. The text is shown in the Annotation Construction window with the same formatting and sizing as the new feature will have when it is placed on the map (the reference scale is not used in the window).

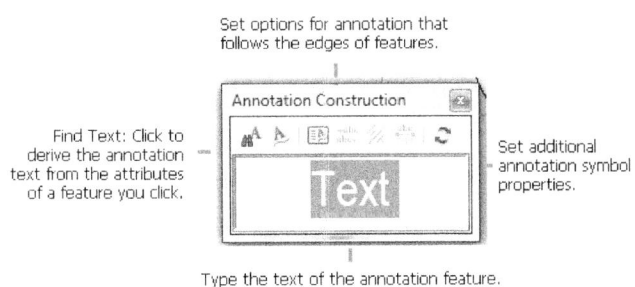

Find Text: Click to derive the annotation text from the attributes of a feature you click.

Set options for annotation that follows the edges of features.

Set additional annotation symbol properties.

Type the text of the annotation feature. It is formatted as it will appear on the map.

The default construction tool is one of the properties of a feature template. When you choose a template on the Create Features window, the default construction tool is activated. For example, if you are creating annotation that identifies the names of roads or rivers, you might want to make the default construction tool be the Follow Feature Annotation tool, which is used to create annotation that follows along the shapes of polygons or lines. To set the properties of a feature template, double-click it in the Create Features window.

When you are creating annotation, you can change the symbol properties for the annotation. If you find that you are making many changes to the symbology, you should consider using or creating a new symbol rather than modifying the symbol extensively.

11.3.3 Convert labels to annotation

3.1 Add the data to your map that will help you determine the best size, placement, and appearance of the labels you want to convert to annotation.

3.2 Zoom to the scale at which you will normally view the annotation regardless of whether you'll view it in ArcMap or on a hard-copy map.

3.3 Right click on the layer, and select "Convert labels to Annotation"

3.4 You will get the "Convert labels to Annotation" dialog box.

3.5 Select "in a database" from store annotation frame, to save your annotation onto your geodatabase.

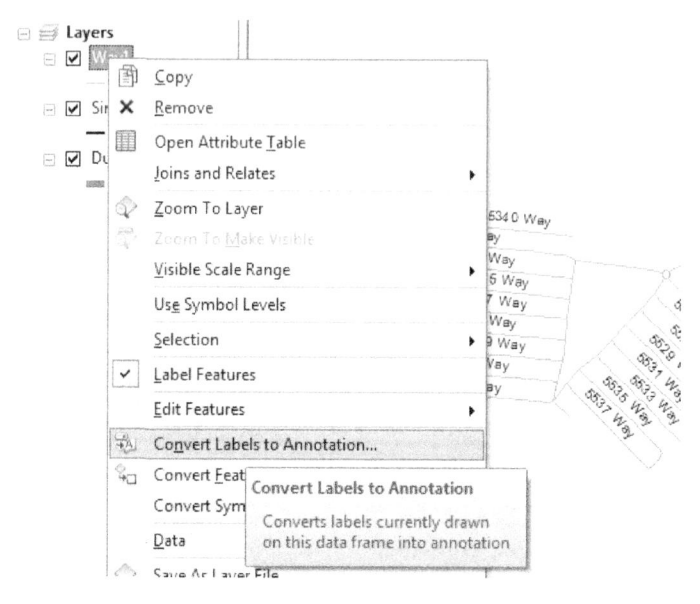

3.6 Select "All features" from "Create annotation for" frame. (To convert labels within a certain extent only, zoom to the extent containing the labels.) And press ok

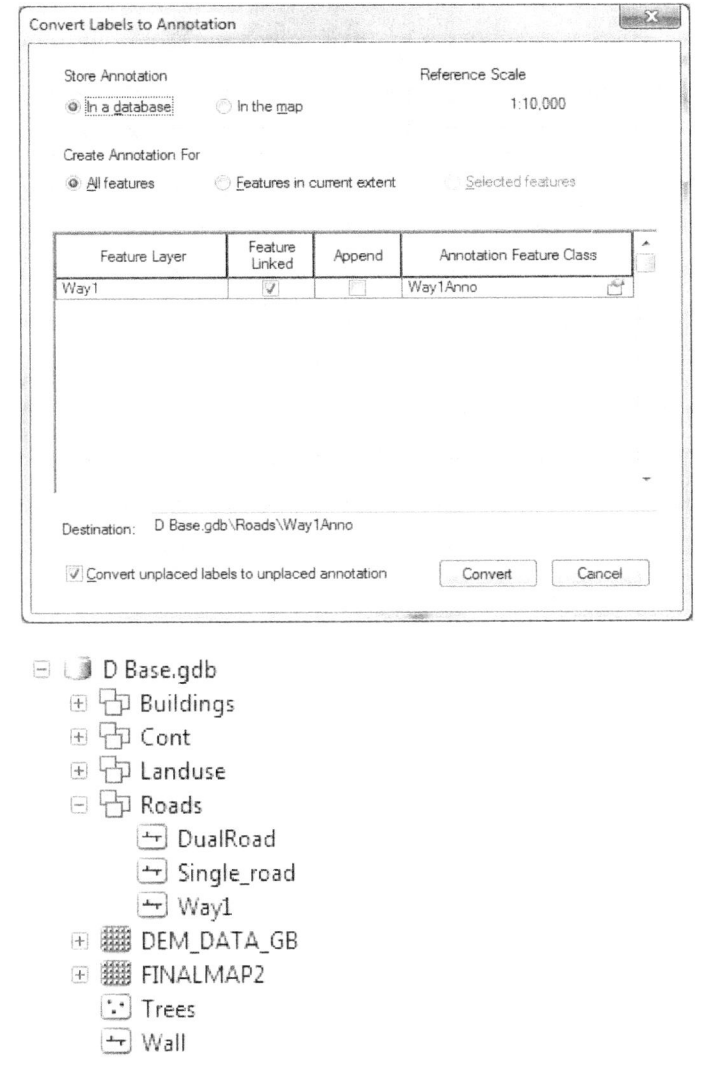

- D Base.gdb
  - Buildings
  - Cont
  - Landuse
  - Roads
    - DualRoad
    - Single_road
    - Way1
  - DEM_DATA_GB
  - FINALMAP2
  - Trees
  - Wall

3.7 Annotation will be created and saved as feature class on the same feature dataset.

12. Network Analyses

12.1 The Network Analyst

Using the Network Analyst extension to ArcGIS for Server, you can publish network analysis tools and datasets to an ArcGIS Server site and expose them in desktop, web, and mobile applications. You can also use the Network Analyst extension to solve advanced routing problems on a central server, such as changing a driving route based on historical or live traffic data, and report the results to clients.

For example, with the Network Analyst extension, you can answer questions like the following:

- What is the quickest way to get from point A to point B?
- Which houses are within five minutes of a fire station?
- What market areas does a business cover?
- Which ambulances or patrol cars can respond quickest to an incident?
- If a company has to downsize, which stores should it close to maintain the most overall demand?

To answer these kinds of questions using the Network Analyst extension, first you need a network dataset, which represents the transportation network. Then you can create network analysis layers on the network dataset and solve them to find solutions to network problems. The network analysis layer contains the parameters, inputs, and outputs for a network problem. There are currently six types of analyses you can perform:

- Route
- Service Area
- Closest Facility
- OD Cost Matrix

- Vehicle Routing Problem
- Location–Allocation

12.2 Network Dataset

Network datasets are well suited to model transportation networks. They are created from source features, which can include simple features (lines and points) and turns, and store the connectivity of the source features. When you perform an analysis using the ArcGIS Network Analyst extension, the analysis always happens on a network dataset.

A network dataset models the street network shown in the graphic below. The graphic highlights that one-way streets, turn restrictions, and overpasses/tunnels can be modeled. The analyses that are performed on the network, such as the route from stop 1 to stop 2, respect these and other network dataset properties.

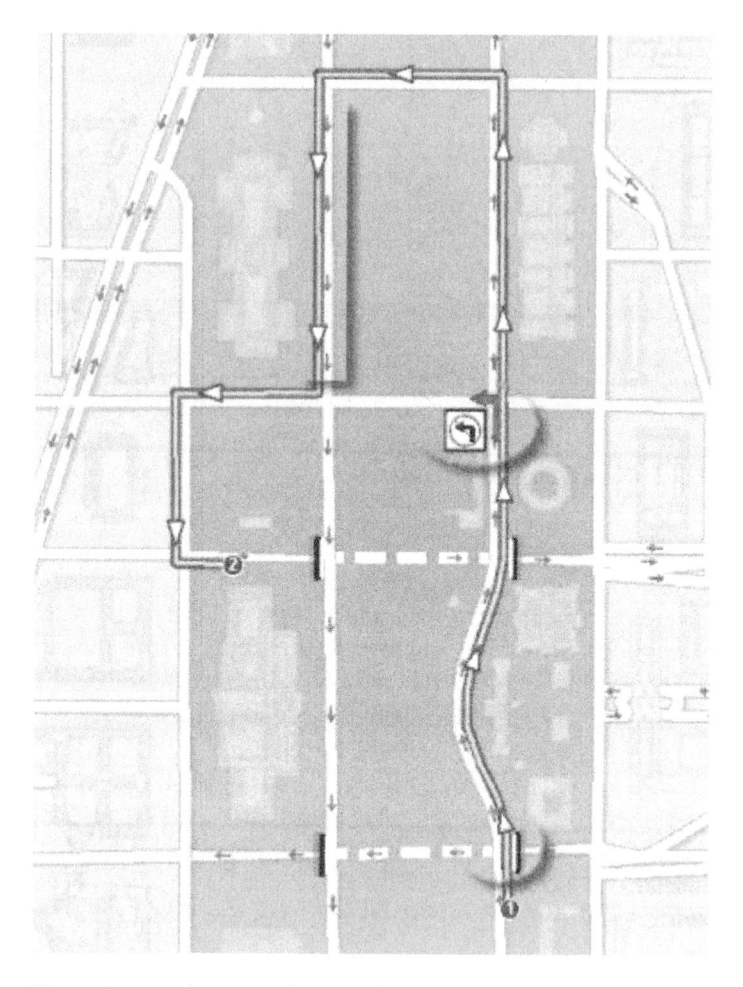

To understand connectivity and why it's important, consider that features are normally unaware of each other. For example, if two line features intersect, neither line is aware of the other. Similarly, a point feature at the end of a line feature doesn't have any inherent information that lets it know about the line. However, the network dataset keeps track of which source features are coincident. It also has a connectivity policy, which you can modify, to further define which coincident features are truly connected. This makes it possible to model overpasses and underpasses without having the roads connect. This way, when a network analysis is performed, the solvers know which paths along the network are feasible.

12.3 Multimodal network dataset

More complex connectivity scenarios, such as multimodal transportation networks, are also possible. The following is an example of a transportation network in downtown Paris displaying road, rail, and bus networks.

The network dataset also possesses a rich network attribute model that helps model impedances, restrictions, and hierarchy for the network.

12.4 Exercise

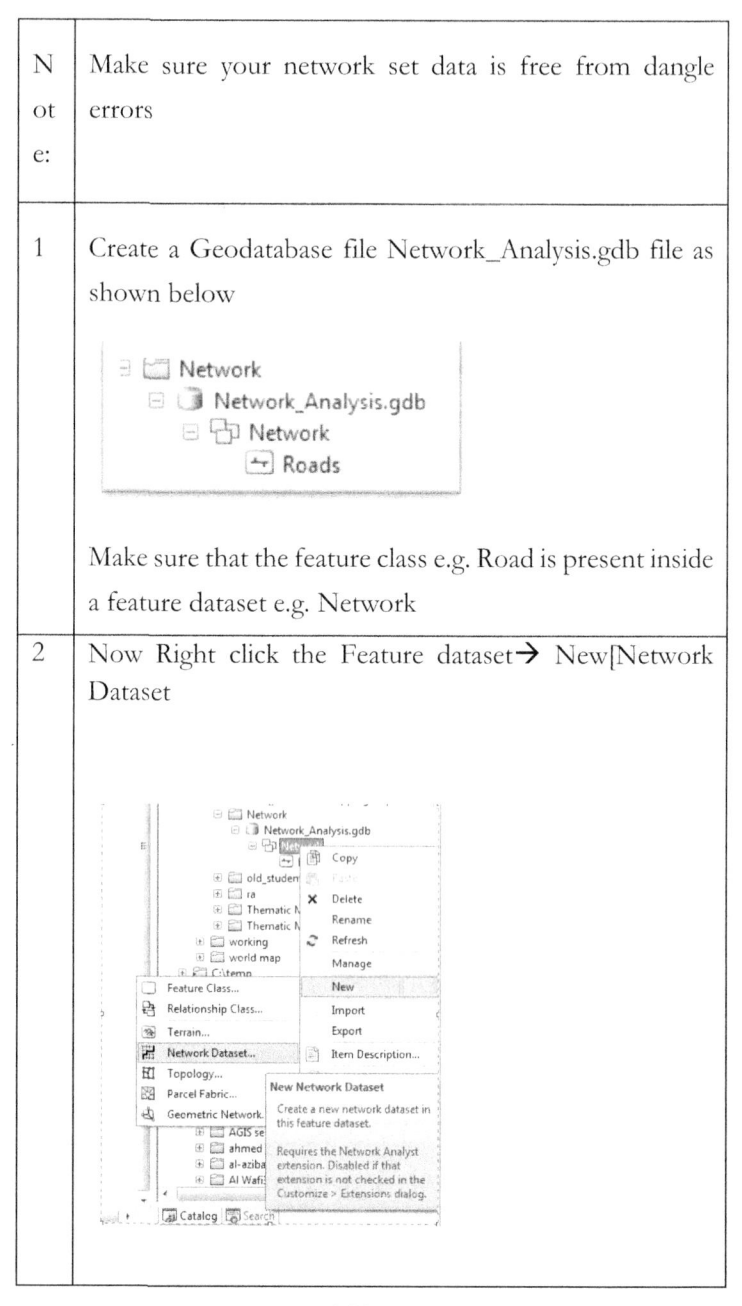

N ot e:	Make sure your network set data is free from dangle errors

1	Create a Geodatabase file Network_Analysis.gdb file as shown below
	
	  Network
	    Network_Analysis.gdb
	      Network
	       Roads
	
	Make sure that the feature class e.g. Road is present inside a feature dataset e.g. Network

2	Now Right click the Feature dataset→ New[Network Dataset

3	
4	

MAPPING IN GIS

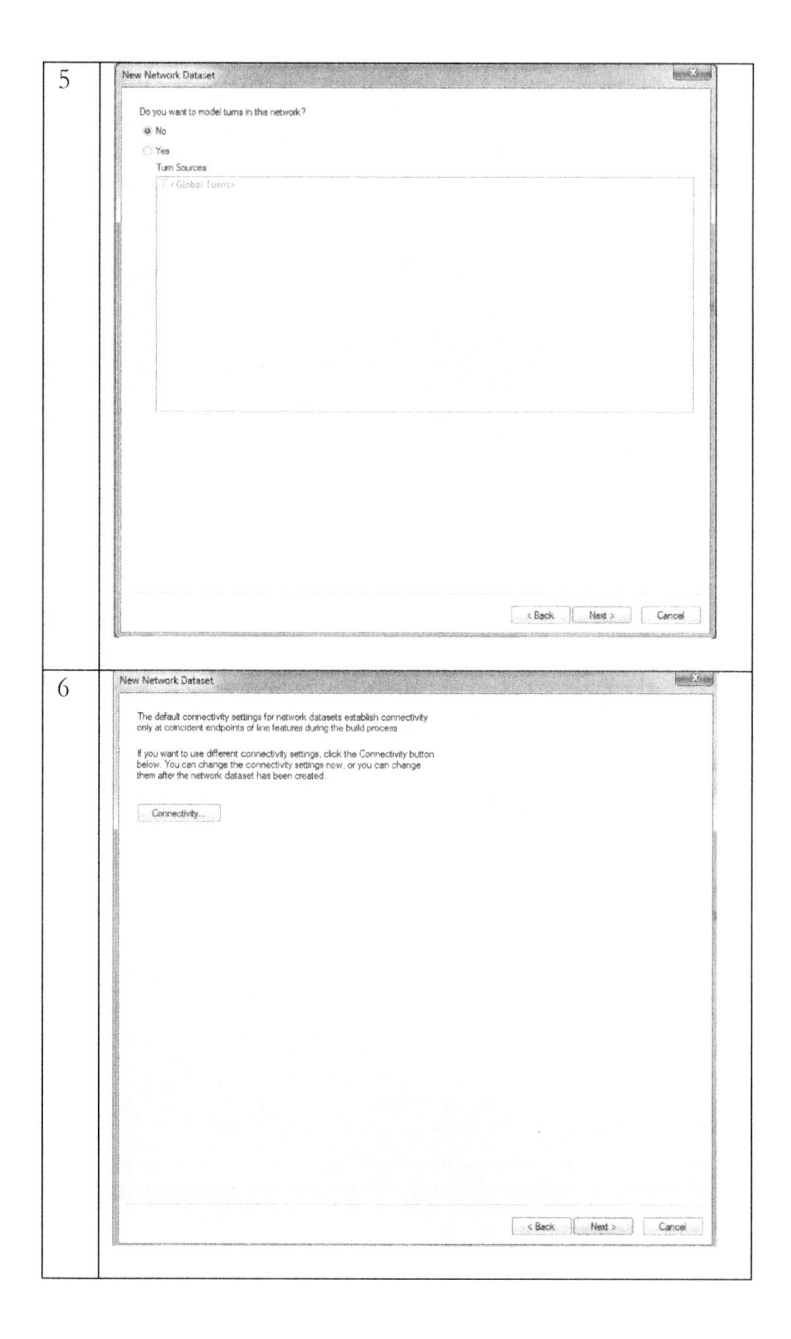

5	**New Network Dataset** Do you want to model turns in this network? ● No ○ Yes Turn Sources: ☑ <Global Turns>
6	**New Network Dataset** The default connectivity settings for network datasets establish connectivity only at coincident endpoints of line features during the build process. If you want to use different connectivity settings, click the Connectivity button below. You can change the connectivity settings now, or you can change them after the network dataset has been created. [Connectivity...]

MAPPING IN GIS

7. New Network Dataset

How would you like to model the elevation of your network features?

● None
○ Using Z Coordinate Values from Geometry
○ Using Elevation Fields

Source	End	Field
Roads	From End	
Roads	To End	

Click in the Field column to set elevation fields.

[< Back] [Next >] [Cancel]

MAPPING IN GIS

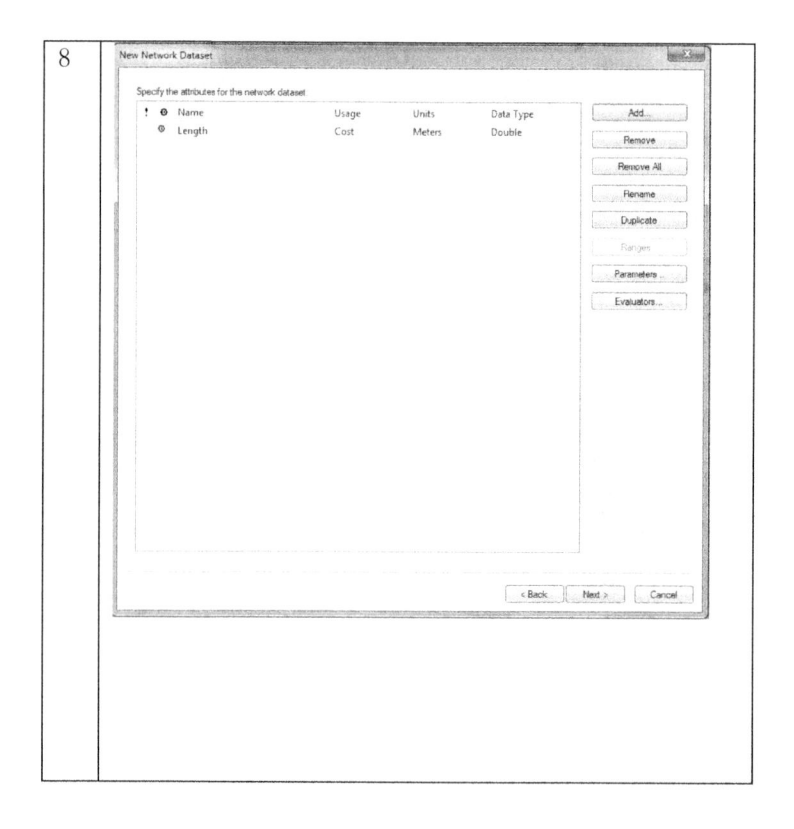

8 | New Network Dataset

Specify the attributes for the network dataset

	Name	Usage	Units	Data Type
	Length	Cost	Meters	Double

Add
Remove
Remove All
Rename
Duplicate
Ranges
Parameters...
Evaluators...

< Back | Next > | Cancel

MAPPING IN GIS

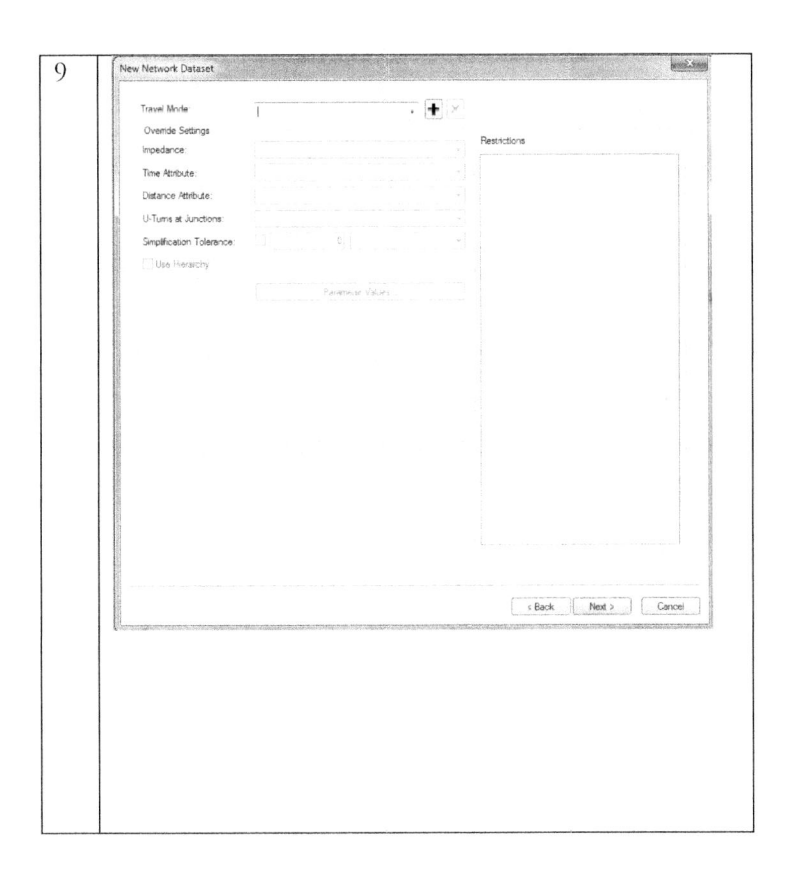

9

MAPPING IN GIS

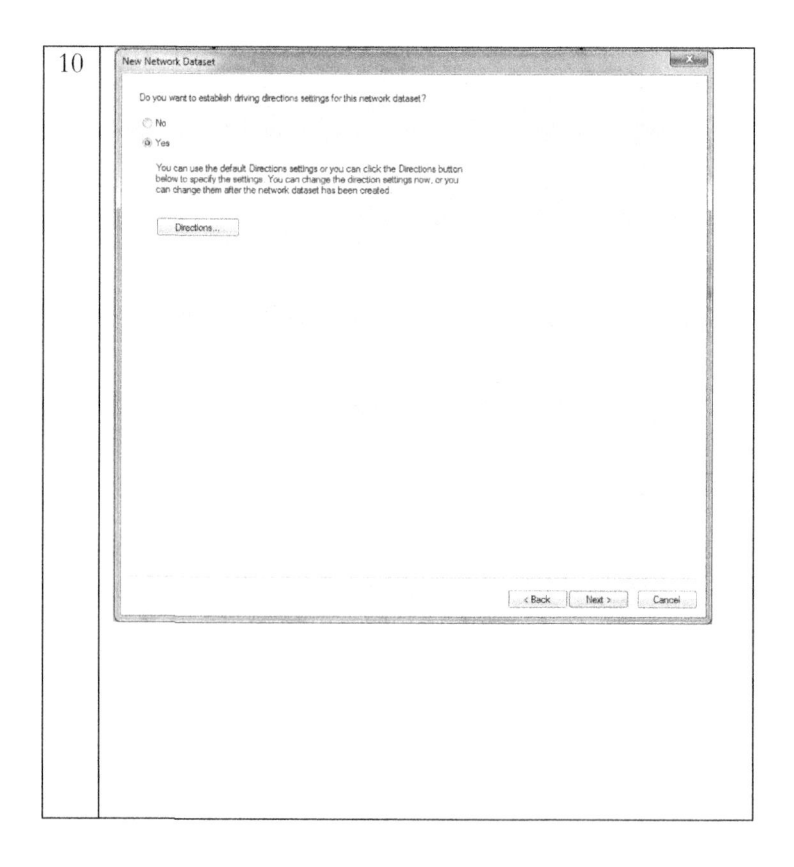

10 | New Network Dataset

Do you want to establish driving directions settings for this network dataset?

○ No
● Yes

You can use the default Directions settings or you can click the Directions button below to specify the settings. You can change the direction settings now, or you can change them after the network dataset has been created.

[Directions...]

[< Back] [Next >] [Cancel]

MAPPING IN GIS

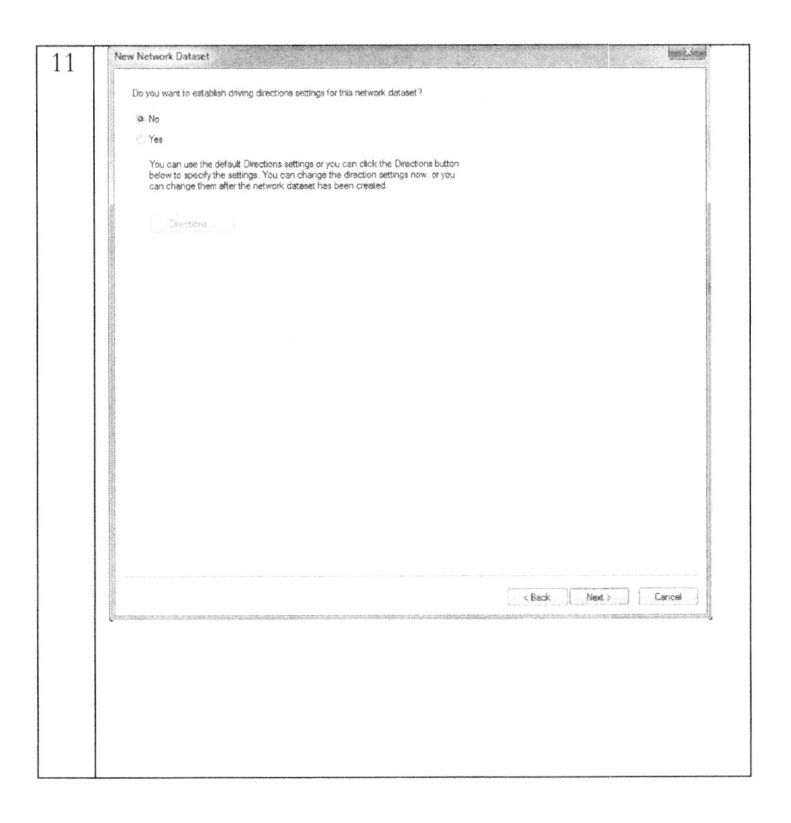

11

New Network Dataset

Do you want to establish driving directions settings for this network dataset?

◉ No
○ Yes

You can use the default Directions settings or you can click the Directions button below to specify the settings. You can change the direction settings now, or you can change them after the network dataset has been created.

[Directions]

[< Back] [Next >] [Cancel]

MAPPING IN GIS

12	New Network Dataset ☐ Build Service Area Index The network dataset will build additional index feature classes that speed Service Area creation. These feature classes will be maintained through incremental rebuild operations. [< Back] [Next >] [Cancel]

13.

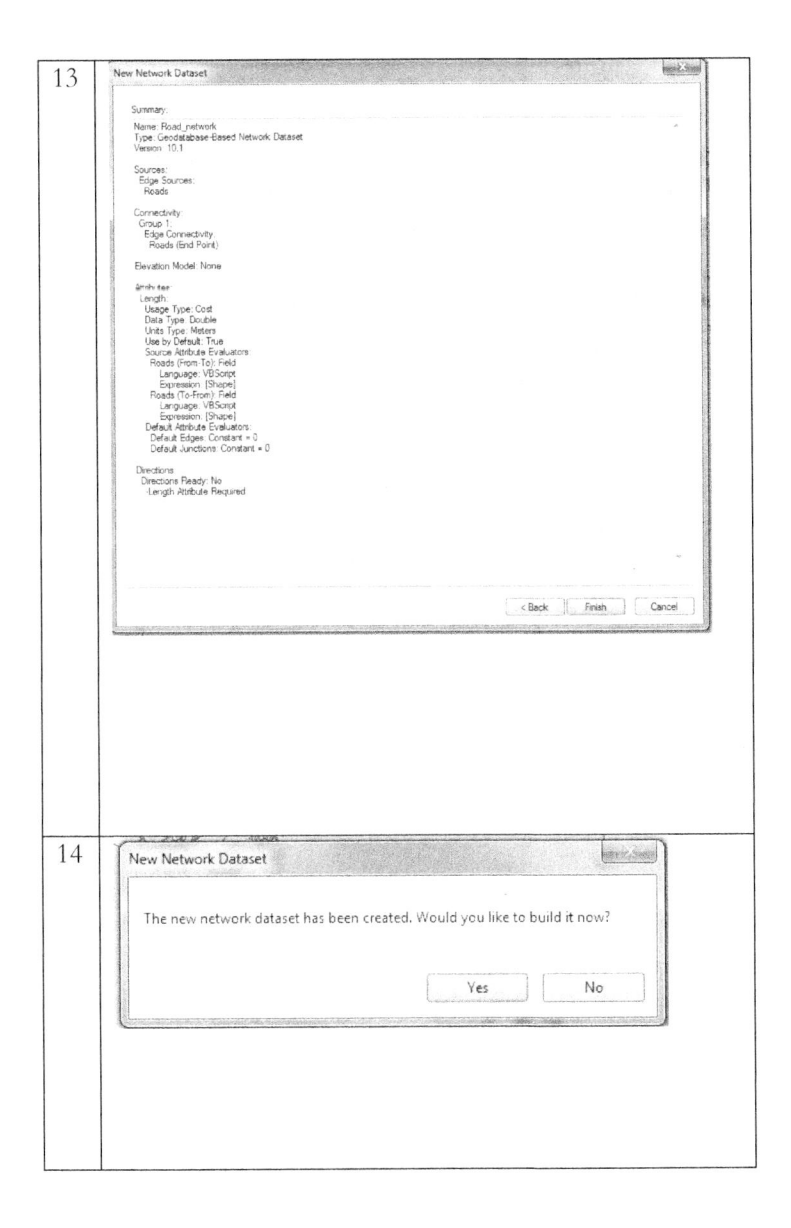

```
New Network Dataset

Summary:

Name: Road_network
Type: Geodatabase-Based Network Dataset
Version: 10.1

Sources:
  Edge Sources:
    Roads

Connectivity:
  Group 1:
    Edge Connectivity:
      Roads (End Point)

Elevation Model: None

Attributes:
  Length:
    Usage Type: Cost
    Data Type: Double
    Units Type: Meters
    Use by Default: True
    Source Attribute Evaluators:
      Roads (From-To): Field
        Language: VBScript
        Expression: [Shape]
      Roads (To-From): Field
        Language: VBScript
        Expression: [Shape]
    Default Attribute Evaluators:
      Default Edges: Constant = 0
      Default Junctions: Constant = 0

Directions:
  Directions Ready: No
  Length Attribute Required

                        < Back    Finish    Cancel
```

14.

```
New Network Dataset

The new network dataset has been created. Would you like to build it now?

                                    Yes         No
```

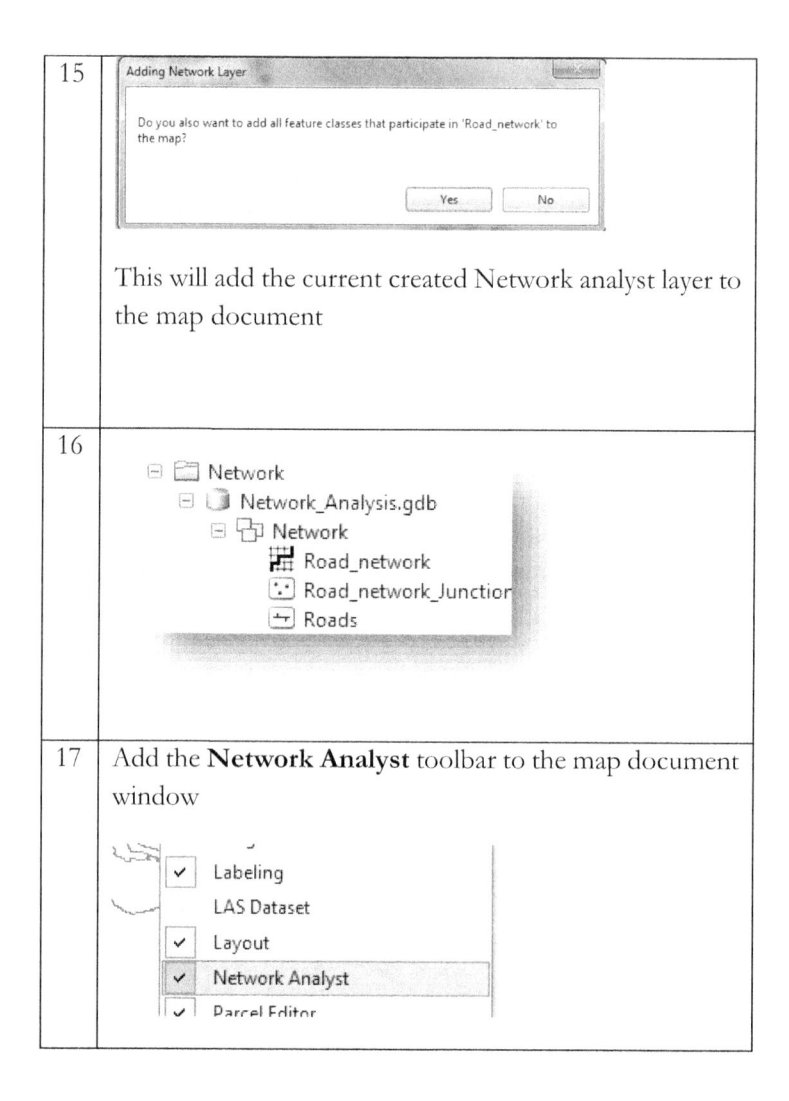

15	*[Adding Network Layer dialog: "Do you also want to add all feature classes that participate in 'Road_network' to the map?" with Yes/No buttons]* This will add the current created Network analyst layer to the map document

16	⊟ 📁 Network
	   ⊟ 🗄 Network_Analysis.gdb
	      ⊟ 🕀 Network
	         🛗 Road_network
	         ⊙ Road_network_Junction
	         ↔ Roads

17	Add the **Network Analyst** toolbar to the map document window ✓ Labeling LAS Dataset ✓ Layout ✓ Network Analyst ✓ Parcel Editor

MAPPING IN GIS

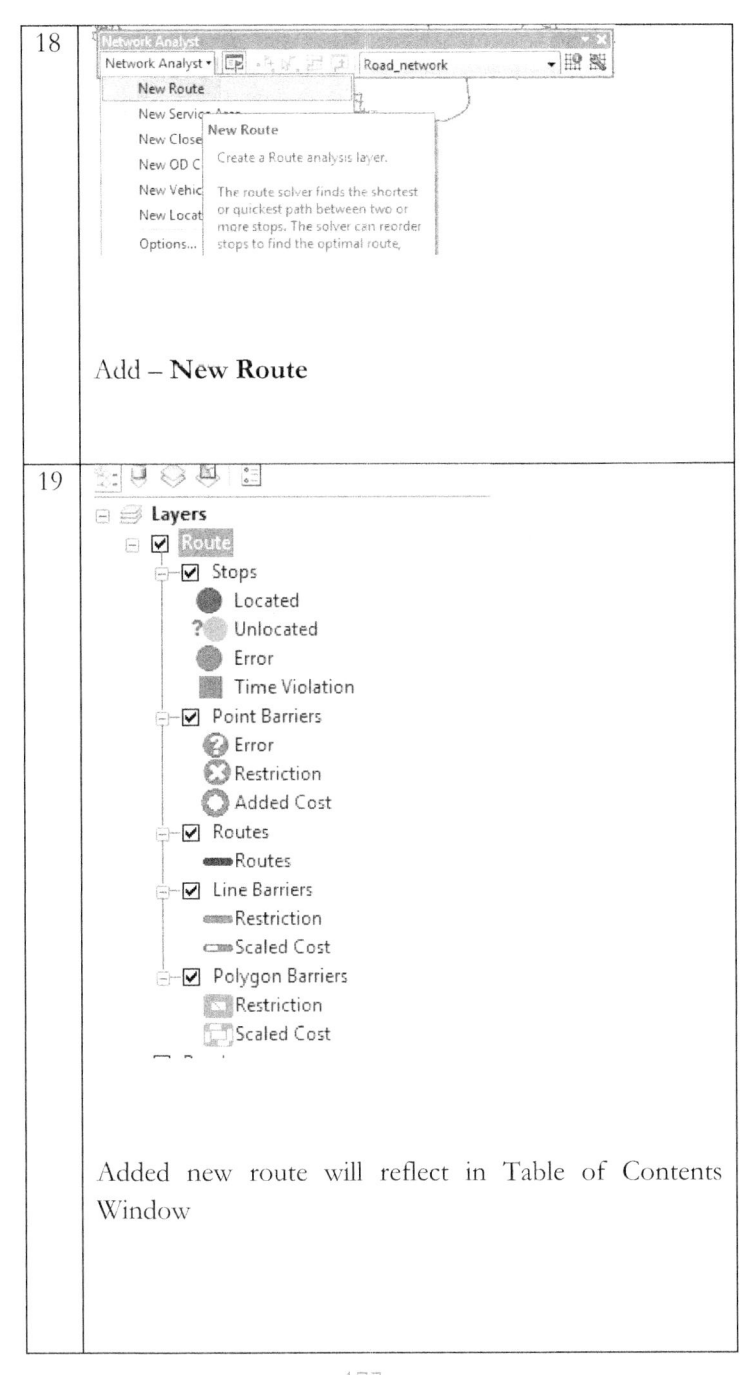

18	Add – **New Route**
19	Added new route will reflect in Table of Contents Window

177

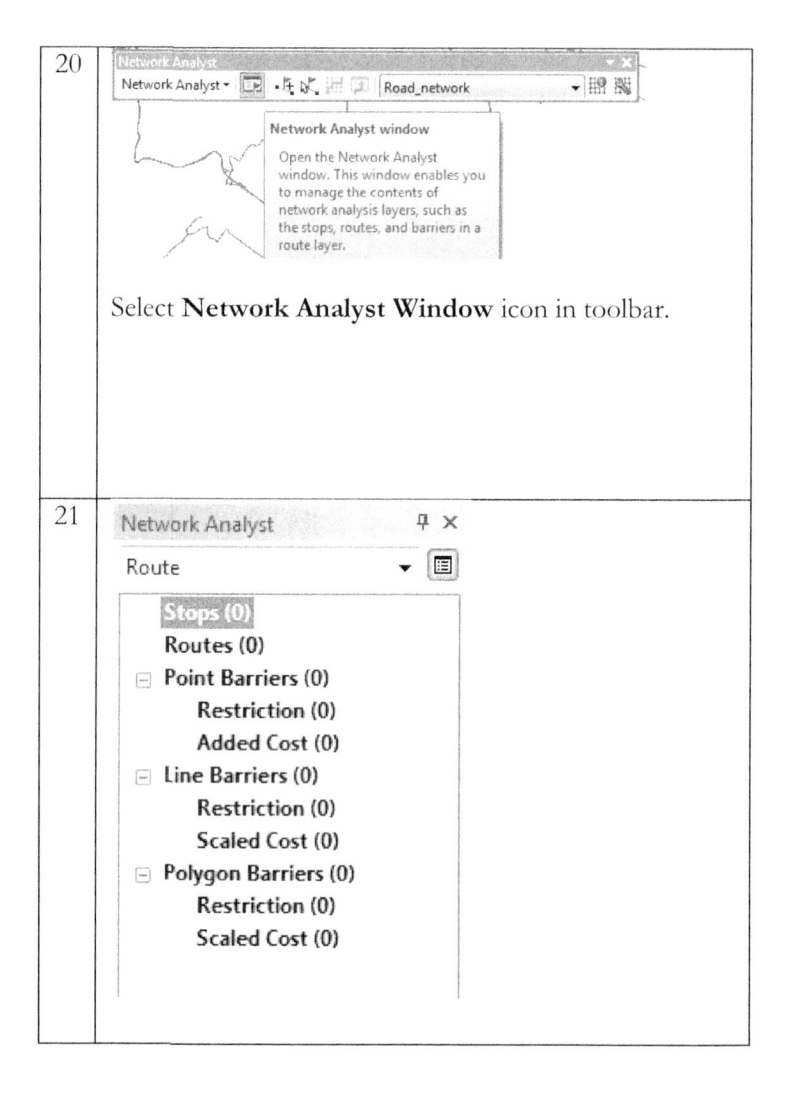

20	Select **Network Analyst Window** icon in toolbar.
21	

MAPPING IN GIS

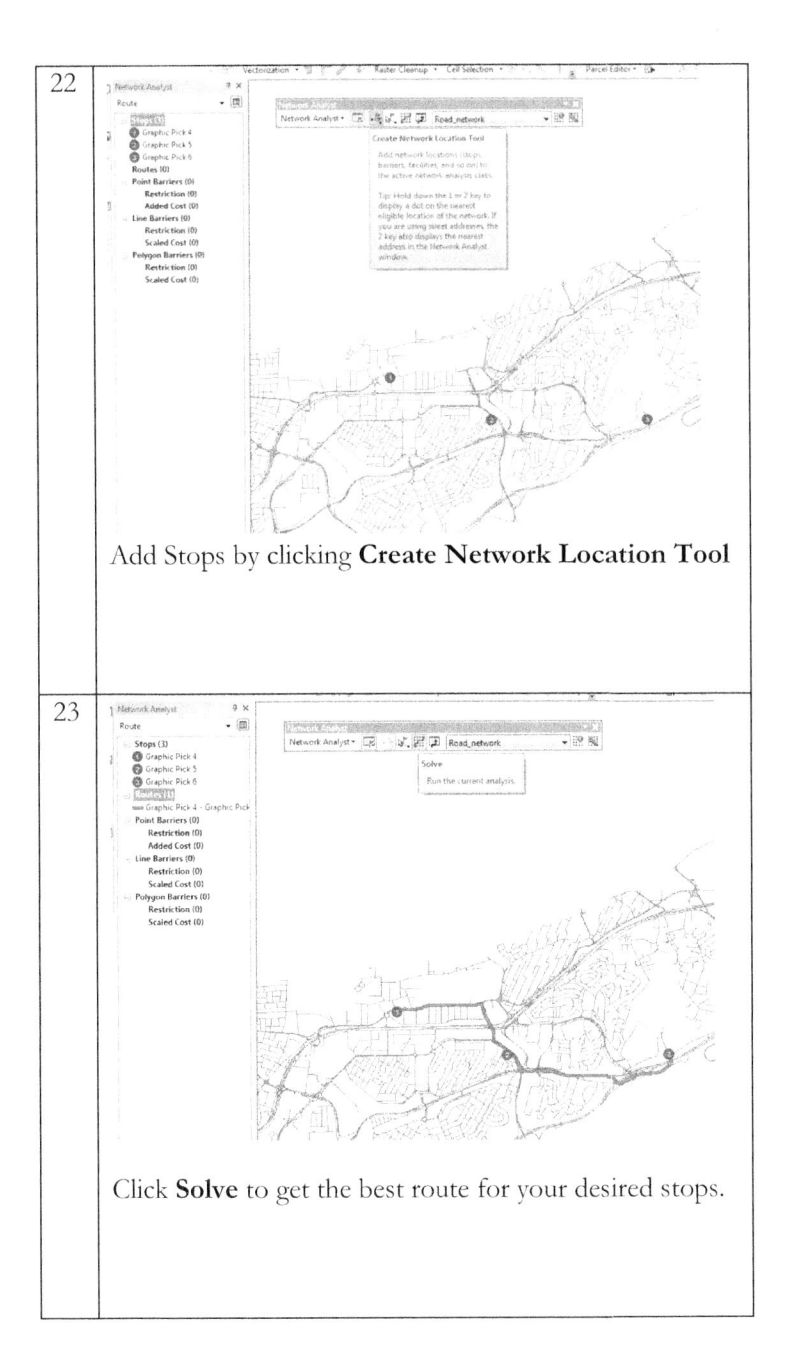

22	Add Stops by clicking **Create Network Location Tool**
23	Click **Solve** to get the best route for your desired stops.

MAPPING IN GIS

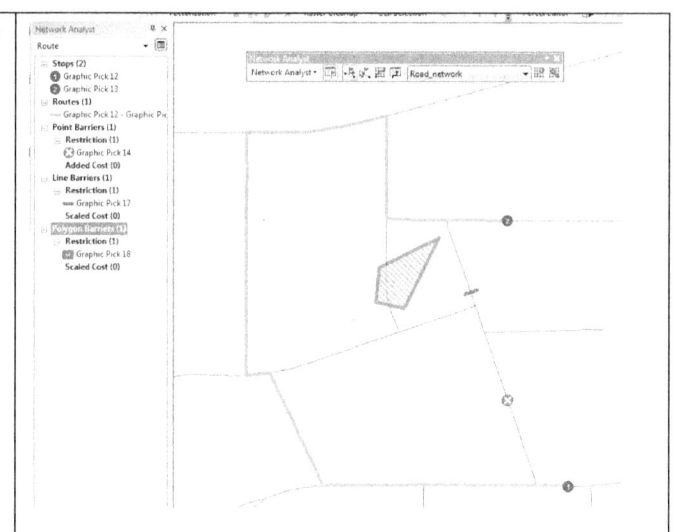

24 | Likewise, you can add hindrances to the network data by adding Point/Line/Polygon Barriers.

(Refer the above image)

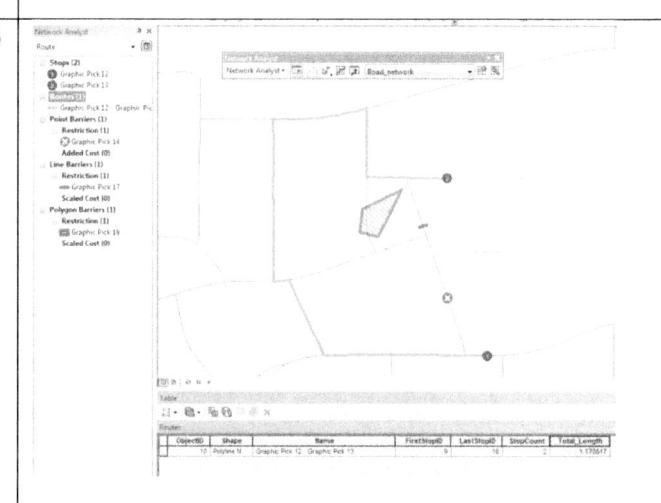

25 | The solved best route is recorded with its attributes.

26	Similarly Network Analysis is useful to solve, • **New Closest Facility** – *e.g. for finding closet fire stations* • **New Service Area** – *e.g. to caluclate distance can be reached from a facility within a specified amount of time.* • **New OD Cost Matrix** – e.g. delivery fo goods from warehouse to stores • **New Vehicle Routing Problem** – e.g. to monitor fleets management • **New Location - Allocation** - *e.g. to choose store locations that would generate most business for retail chain.*